NO
IS A
FOUR-
LETTER
WORD

HOW I FAILED SPELLING
BUT SUCCEEDED IN LIFE

CHRIS JERICHO

DA CAPO PRESS

This book is dedicated to all of you with a dream!
Don't listen to people who say you can't make it happen . . .
because I'm living proof that YOU CAN.

This book is also dedicated to Lemmy.
Pirate. Rebel. Philosopher. Friend.

First Da Capo Press edition 2017
ISBN 978-0-306-82505-7 (hardcover)
ISBN 978-0-306-82506-4 (ebook)

Published by Da Capo Press, an imprint of Perseus Books, LLC,
a subsidiary of Hachette Book Group, Inc.
www.dacapopress.com

Library of Congress Cataloging-in-Publication Data is available for this book.

Editorial production by Christine Marra, *Marra*thon Production Services.
www.marrathoneditorial.org

Design by Jane Raese
Set in 12-point Avance

LSC-C
10 9 8 7 6 5 4 3 2 1

CONTENTS

FOREWORD

Anything is possible if it IS truly possible.

With few exceptions, we all know our limitations and what we are capable of achieving.

What stands in the way of reaching our goals is our own self-doubt—self-doubt too often rooted in the voices and actions of the naysayers, whose own failures make them feel threatened by the possibility of you succeeding.

Chris Irvine BECAME Chris Jericho. Not overnight and not without obstacles. Though repeatedly told that he was too short to be a wrestler, he was undeterred.

Show me someone of any height who is motivated by self-determination and self-belief and I'll show you an unstoppable giant.

While it's too simplistic to think that someone can tell you how you, too, can become successful, it can nonetheless be a source of inspiration to find your path by knowing how others have found theirs. And in Chris's case, he is a bright and funny guy whose "can do" spirit and appreciation for his own success makes him the kind of person you want to know.

Positivity breeds positivity.

Enjoy.

Paul Stanley
KISS

INTRODUCTION

NO
IS A
FOUR-
LETTER
WORD

LET'S GET IT STARTED IN HERE!

No, no, no, don't say you can't when you can . . .
—KISS, "NO, NO, NO"

A prerequisite of being a heavy metal kid in the 1980s was watching music videos, and one of the first bands that effectively utilized this new medium to the highest degree was Twisted Sister. TS filmed mini-movie intros to their videos that set the stage for the song, and the best example of this was the prelude for their 1984 monster hit "We're Not Gonna Take It." The video opened with a kid playing air guitar in his room (a ritual that I was also guilty of at the time), until the kid's militant dad (I recognized him instantly as Niedermeyer from *Animal House*) bursts into the room and berates him for wasting his time in hoping that his

1

rock 'n' roll dreams come true. Towering over his son, he gives him the bollocking of his young life, and then demands to know the answer to one simple question:

"WHAT DO YOU WANNA DO WITH YOUR LIFE??"

The kid looks sheepishly up at his parental torturer and barks back (in Dee Snider's voice) these three magic words:

"I WANNA ROCK!"

Then he strums a majestic power chord on his axe and blows his dad out of the second-story window as the song's iconic drum intro kicks in. While I never caused my dad great bodily harm by torpedoing him out of a second-floor window, I do remember having a similar answer when he asked me what I wanted to do with my life.

However, in my case the answer was a little more detailed. Yes, I wanted to rock . . . but I also wanted to wrestle.

You see, I decided when I was twelve years old that I loved both of these equally and therefore was going to succeed at both. I never thought about what the odds were in making it in even one of these vocations, never mind the two of them. But I also didn't care. All I knew was that I wanted to rock and wrestle and wasn't interested in much else.

Well, here we are thirty-five years later in 2017 and lo and behold, good golly Miss Molly—here I am living both my dreams at the highest of levels. Now, even though my success in wrestling is obviously bigger than my success with Fozzy, my band has done a damn good job fighting our way into the big leagues as well. We aren't KISS or Metallica, but we've toured with both and held our own, so I'd say that's pretty freakin' good, wouldn't you agree?

If you do, your million-dollar question might be, "How did you achieve both of your dreams?" Well, for a long time I didn't really have a specific answer; I wanted to be a rocker and wrestler, so I did it. But when the idea of this book was pitched to me by my marvelous literary agent, Marc Gerald, I realized there was a whole lot more to the story of how I got to where I am today than I originally thought.

After much deliberation, I was able to distill the secret of my success (and I ain't talkin' about Michael J. Fox) into twenty simple principles, or rules if you wheeel, that can help you achieve your dreams too. Whether you're looking to get a promotion, land a certain gig, meet the girl or guy of your dreams, or become the first-ever undisputed world champion (actually, scratch that last one, I beat you to it), I think this book will help you.

One of the first things I came up with was the title. It popped into my head early on in the process, because the lesson contained within those six words is fundamental to everything I've achieved. The secret is simple, because "no" really is a four-letter word. Those two runes combined form the most crippling weapon in the English language, an idiom so evil that it has the power to derail even the most dedicated of people and crush their dreams in a split second. It's a word even more repugnant than the most abrasive of profanities, and my whole life I've wanted nothing to do with it.

And let me clarify: this isn't about not taking no for an answer from the girl you want to invite to the sock hop or take out for dinner at the El Pollo Loco. I've accepted those type of no's more times than I'd like to admit. What I'm talking about is not accepting no for an answer when it comes to what you want out of your life and career—that's the kind of no I've never bowed down to. And that's where the idea to write this tome came from.

This book started as a list of twenty lessons I've learned that have guided me through my life and career. Some have more importance than others depending on the moral, and others didn't make the final cut because they just weren't exciting enough to write about (you'll have to wait for volume two to read *The Bob Backlund Principle: Save Your Money*).

Some of the axioms in this *vade mecum* were learned from my parents, others came from various mentors along the way, and others were taught the hardest way of all: by trying, failing, learning, and doing better the next time. My list of rules comes from different sources for sure, but all of them combined form a cohesive philosophy. I know these dictums have helped me immensely in my life, and I'm certain they can help you too.

Now, it's not like you're going to be reading the Dead Sea Scrolls or the *Necronomicon*, but if a few of these chapters influence your life in a positive way and help you become a happier person, then both of us will have gained something.

This is my motivational book. There are many motivational books like it, but this one is mine. My motivational book is my best friend. It is my life. I must master it as I master my life. Without me, my motivational book is useless and without my motivational book, I am useless, ya dig?

All right, enough of my yacking. It's time to turn the page (and I ain't talkin' about Bob Seger) and get started. LET'S BOOGIE!

CHAPTER 1

THE MIKE DAMONE PRINCIPLE

WHEREVER YOU ARE, THAT'S THE PLACE TO BE

The chance you got comes never twice,
do your best (and) do it right . . .
—HELLOWEEN, "THE CHANCE"

Mike Damone is one of the coolest characters in cinematic history and if you don't agree, well then, you don't know Jack . . . or should I say Mike.

What I'm saying is if you haven't seen *Fast Times at Ridgemont High*, I highly recommend that you check it out, as the story and characters are flawless. For those of you cool cats who have seen it, you might be more familiar with Sean Penn's Jeff Spicoli ("Awesome. Totally awesome!") or Judge Reinhold's Brad Hamilton ("I hope you had a hell of a piss, Arnold!"), but the quote I always identified with the most was by Robert Romanus's Mike Damone.

Damone was a Fonz-esque ne'er-do-well who would just as easily swindle you for overpriced scalped Earth, Wind & Fire tickets as he would give you sagelike life advice. He walked the face of the mall doling out nuggets of straight fire to his nerdy protégé, Mark Ratner, on a number of subjects, especially on how to pick up girls. When Rat is having problems figuring out a way to break the ice with his high school crush, Stacy (who Damone ends up banging in a pool cabana), Mike gives him a bunch of tips on how to make it happen. Having attitude and confidence, ordering for the lady in the restaurant, and making out to *Led Zeppelin IV* are all on this magic list, but it's his next tip that stood out the most, because it applies to a whole lot more than just picking up Stacy Hamilton.

"Wherever you are, that's the place to be," Mike proclaims as he majestically surveys his surroundings, spreading out his arms regally with a giant grin on his face.

"Isn't this GREAT?" he continues joyously.

It's a brilliant piece of advice that can be used in all situations, because what Damone is saying is that no matter what you're doing or where you are, you need to act like it's the best place on earth and make the best of what you're given.

Now, for example, if you take Damone's words and apply them to an assignment given to you by your boss (no matter how big or small), imagine how much more fire you will have to get it done! In my lines of work, it can be frustrating to only have a few minutes on *Raw* or a short set at a rock festival to show the crowd what I've got. But much like a fourth-line player on a great hockey team, if you perform that smaller role well, your team will win and you'll probably get a bigger role next time.

When I last saw you, Constant Reader, at the end of my third magnum opus, *The Best in the World: At What I Have No Idea*, I had just been announced in the 2013 Royal Rumble as a surprise entrant. It was one of my favorite WWE moments, as it was a legit surprise for the sold-out crowd in Phoenix, and they went totally ballistic when I walked onto the stage.

That Rumble appearance was going to be the beginning of a multi-month storyline that would lead to me working against Ryback at WrestleMania 29. While that might not seem like such a big deal now, in 2013 it would've been a big match.

At the time, Ryback's star had risen to where I feel if he had won the world title, the WWE Universe would've bought into it big time. He was so over that I even imagined a scenario where he would win the WWE Championship from CM Punk in October and go on to face The Undertaker in April at WrestleMania 29. Facing Taker at the biggest show of the year was a huge honor— the Holy Grail even—and I felt with his push and current momentum that The Big Guy was explosive and powerful enough to be a formidable Mania dance partner for The Deadman.

For whatever reason, things didn't go that way. Ryback lost to Punk and didn't win the world championship. But he was still over in a big way, and I thought a great way to build him back up again would be to work with me. When I pitched the story to the creative team for me to come back for a six-month run through Mania ending at SummerSlam, my two tent-pole ideas were a surprise return at the Rumble and a Mania match with Ryback.

After I returned, I worked the first few months against random opponents, including an Elimination Chamber match that was so uneventful I had to google it to remember who else was in it. I figured that my angle with Ryback would begin shortly after, as the road to WrestleMania always started the day after the Chamber PPV. But it didn't and Ryback seemed to be moving toward a storyline with Mark Henry. That confused me because even though my match had already been approved by my boss, Vince McMahon, I wasn't hearing anything about it from anybody. Finally, I called head writer Dave Kapoor to find out what was going down. It turned out my suspicion was correct.

"Ryback is going to work with Mark Henry at Mania," Dave told me, "but don't worry, Vince has something else planned for you, and he wants to tell you about it himself."

I appreciated his candor and wondered what Vince had up his sleeve. Four years earlier, he had worked out a deal with Mickey Rourke (who was riding a massive career resurgence from his Oscar-nominated role in *The Wrestler*) to have a match with me at WrestleMania 25, and even though that match never happened, I still ended up in a pretty good spot working against three WWE Hall of Famers in Roddy Piper, Ricky Steamboat, and Jimmy Snuka . . . and getting knocked out by Rourke at the end. I was excited and wondered what featured role the boss had in mind for me this time around.

I waited a few weeks for him to give me the heads-up, but he never did. I prodded Kapoor to give me a clue, but he insisted that he didn't know anything. I promised myself I wouldn't give in and ask Vince what he had in mind (giving him the upper hand), but with all the other Mania programs already full steam ahead, I started wondering if I was even going to be on the show at all. With just over a month until the big night, all of the top names in the company had already been paired off, along with most of the mid-card guys (except a new character with these goofy vignettes on *Raw*, but there was no way I'd be working with him). I assumed Vince had lined up another outside celebrity, but I'd been racking my brain and had absolutely no idea who it might be.

I couldn't take it anymore, so I shot Vince a text and said: I HEAR YOU'VE GOT A SECRET PLAN FOR ME AT MANIA. LIBERACE IN A TUXEDO MATCH? SY SPERLING IN A HAIR VS HAIR? WHEN ARE YOU PLANNING ON FILLING ME IN?

Vince texted me back a few minutes later and said something along the lines of: YOU THINK YOU'RE WORKING A MATCH AT MANIA? I THOUGHT I'D JUST HAVE YOU SET UP THE RING.

Uh-oh.

The fact that Vince was dodging my question behind the veil of a bad joke wasn't a good sign, and I told him so.

Thirty minutes later my phone rang and I saw vkm on the screen. When I answered, Vince was being over-the-top charming, littering his speech with more bad jokes and fake laughs. It felt like he was trying to butter me up before telling me something I wouldn't like.

Yowzah, was I right.

"Well, I know we talked about you and Ryback, but I want to go in a different direction. I have another idea for you."

I waited in silence for him to continue. The pause was intentionally uncomfortable and Vince continued in a serious tone.

"We have this new kid called Fandango . . ."

WHAT??

Fandango was the character I'd thought about earlier, whose goofy *Dancing with the Stars*–themed gimmick had been promoted for weeks on TV with a bunch of campy vignettes.

"He's a good worker and I really believe in this gimmick. I'd like to have him debut at WrestleMania, and I can't think of a bigger and better opponent for him than . . . CHRIS JERICHO!" Vince proclaimed boisterously like a jacked-up P. T. Barnum, using his famed McJedi mind tricks to try to convince me that this was the opportunity of a lifetime.

I lost all sense of decorum and lashed out way too harshly at my billionaire boss.

"Are you kidding me?? You're gonna put me in the ring with FANDANGO at WrestleMania? You agreed to have me work with Ryback and now you're pairing me with a guy who hasn't even been on TV yet?"

"This gimmick is going to be big and I need to debut him with a bang, Chris! Get in there with him, take 90 percent of the match, and go straight to the finish."

It didn't surprise me that Vince thought that the character was going to be big, because I knew exactly where he came up with the idea. A few years prior when I was on *DWTS*, Vince called to tell me how proud he was that I was doing the show. We were talking about how intense the rehearsals and training were and I mentioned how in shape the male dancers were.

"Oh, there's no doubt about that," he said, "but they look ridiculous dancing and prancing across the floor. How can you ever take them seriously?"

At that moment, I knew it wouldn't be long before there was a character based on a male ballroom dancer, and here he was. This reminded me of when I predicted a "heel wearing a scarf" character after Vince mocked me for consistently wearing one. (Scarves are cool, and if they're good enough for Keith Richards, they're good enough for me.) Sure enough, a few weeks later Alberto Del Rio was walking to the ring wearing one of his own. (I've since reclaimed the scarf heat for my own act.)

But despite Vince's suggestion of squashing Fandango, I still wasn't happy about the idea and tried to give him some other options.

"What if I challenge Wade Barrett for the Intercontinental Championship instead? We could come up with a story where I'm chasing my self-record-breaking tenth IC title by trying to beat my former protégé."

I had been Barrett's mentor on the inaugural season of the original *NXT* show, which was based around eight "rookies" being advised by their individual "pros," and Wade was my rookie so the angle was a no-brainer. Vince didn't agree.

"Oh come on, nobody remembers that. Besides, this Fandango character is a real heat magnet and the kid has a ton of personality. This is the way to go."

Vince was right in the fact that Johnny Curtis, who was playing Fandango, was charismatic and a good worker. I just didn't think debuting him at Mania against me was best for My business. But alas, I knew the battle had been lost.

"It doesn't matter what I say at this point does it, Vince? This is the way you want it and nothing I say is going to change your mind, is it?"

"No. This what I want."

"Whatever," I spit out and hung up on him.

I was pissed off and felt double-crossed by Vince. When I called Kapoor and told him that my Mania opponent was going to be Fandango, even he couldn't hide his surprise.

"Wow," was his one-word answer that said more than a thousand words could have.

I was caught somewhere in time, mad as hell and thought about simply refusing to do the match. Vince had no right to treat me this way, and broken promises didn't sit well with me, especially when that meant I was going to be saddled in a prelim match at the biggest show of the year. What should I do? Where should I turn? Who could give me the advice I needed to make the right decision? There was only one man wise enough for that.

The Undertaker.

I called and told him of my conundrum. He listened to my concerns and then calmly gave his analysis.

"Listen, man, I know how you are feeling right now, but let's be honest. Either you do the match or you quit. And you'd be stupid to quit, because this really isn't that bad. I know everybody talks about my WrestleMania winning streak [which at the time was 20–0], and over the last few years those matches have been pretty damn good, but they weren't always that way. Vince put me in there with a lot of dudes who weren't exactly easy to work with [he mentioned no names, but guys like Giant Gonzalez, King Kong Bundy, and a way past his prime Jimmy Snuka crossed my mind], but I did the best I could with what I was given because it was MY JOB. It was Vince's call and I did what he wanted. So take this opportunity Vince is giving you, do your best, and make it good. If you do that, he will take care of you. Honestly, Chris, this is part of your job . . . so go do it."

Everything he said was right, and deep down inside I knew it. I just needed to hear it from him and once I did, it was all systems go (and I ain't talkin' about the Vinnie Vincent Invasion) with no looking back. This was my mission and I was going to accept it and do everything I could to get both Fandango and the angle over as much as possible in the short amount of time I had.

My first thought was I needed to get the fans familiar with the Fandango character as quickly as I could, and the best way to do that was to mess with his name so they would recognize it. So in our first meeting, I decided to mispronounce it in as many ways as I could think of. When he made his debut appearance on *Raw* by interrupting me in the middle of a backstage promo, I asked him his name and he replied, "Faaan . . . Dahn . . . Go."

I stared at him in silence until he said it again, and then I tried to repeat it.

"Faan . . . Dum . . . Bo."

He corrected me and said his name again.

"Faaan . . . Dahn . . . Go!"

"FanDunghole."

He had a conniption fit and repeated his moniker for a third time.

I proceeded to beat the dead dancing horse by throwing out a litany of butchered attempts to get it right.

"Fandjango, Fandangle, FanDodgeDurango, FanSweetMango, FanWangoTango, Fan-Dingo-Ate-My-Baby-O" (that was my personal favorite), and finally:

"Fan-B-I-N-G-O-Was-His-Name-O."

Instantly, we established his name and the fact that I couldn't (or refused to) pronounce it correctly. It gave me and the fans something to sink our teeth into right off the bat, which the angle desperately needed.

The next step was to get him over as a serious threat. With a gimmick that campy, it would be easy to dismiss him as a joke, and I didn't want that happening on my watch. Fandango was a good worker with a great top-rope legdrop for a finish, so I worked on getting that over. It was an impressive-looking move, and I had him nail me with it every time he attacked me for the next few weeks.

Even when the plan was for me to get one up on him, I changed it to him beating me up and hitting me with the legdrop again. Everybody knew me and my moves, but nobody had seen what this dancing fool could do, and we had to establish that he was dangerous.

Over the next few weeks, it was basically a rotating pattern of Fandango beating me down (always culminating with the top-rope legdrop) combined with me mispronouncing his name. It wasn't much, but it was all we had, and in the end it did the trick because by the time we got to Mania, there was interest in the match. Not huge, but more than I was expecting due to a combination of my strategy, Fandango's kitschy character, and his catchy *I Dream of Jeannie*–style entrance music. Some fans were even starting to dance along with his theme song, moving their arms up and down in time with the game show–themed jam while humming along with the melody.

So I took solace in the fact that some fans were looking forward to the match, and even though others thought it was a waste of time, well, it didn't matter anyway since I was winning.

Or was I?

A few days before Mania, producer Dean Malenko called to tell me (much to my shock) that the finish was Fandango going over clean, and I went berserk. I called Vince and started screaming that I was sick of this double-crossing bullshit! It was bad enough that he had changed my Mania match to Fandango, but now he was changing the finish too?

Vince seemed genuinely surprised at that last comment.

"I never changed the finish," he replied calmly.

"Are you kidding me? Yes you did!" I bellowed. "You told me to take 90 percent of the match and go straight to the finish!"

"That's what I said."

Then I realized he was right, that was EXACTLY what he said. I thought back to our initial phone conversation when he explained how he wanted the match—a verdict that I had just repeated to him verbatim.

Vince said that he wanted me to "take 90 percent of the match" (aka eat Fandango up and get most of the offense) and then "go straight to the finish." While he never said outright that he wanted Fandango to go over, all I had to do was use the common sense I'd learned after twenty-three years in the business to figure out that if Vince was high enough on Fandango to book him in his first match with me at WrestleMania, there was no way he'd have him lose. I had stuck my patent-leather boot in my mouth by assuming I was going to go over, and we all know what happens when you ASSUME—it makes an ASS out of UME. Now, I'm not sure who in the hell this UME is, but you get the point.

I told Vince that nobody in the audience would buy Fandango beating me clean, but that was precisely what he was counting on.

"That's what I want. I'd be thrilled if seventy-five thousand people started chanting 'bullshit' at the finish. The less they buy it, the better. I wanna really piss them off."

I was still a little pissed off myself, but now that I knew the finish and understood the reason for it, I hunkered down and strategized on how to make the best of it. I had no interest in taking 90 percent of the bout, because I couldn't think of a more boring scenario than a Chris Jericho squash match at Mania, even with a twist ending, so I put the match together with the idea that Fandango could beat me at any time. That worked great because at that point, nobody in their right mind thought I was going to lose that match, and I used that to my advantage to put together the most exciting contest possible.

The match ended up being . . . not bad. Not a classic by any means, but a good second match on the show. The finish would have me go for a lionsault, but Dango would put up his knees. However, I would land on my feet and try for the walls, but he would small-package me for the duke. It didn't go as smoothly as I would've liked, as I overshot him on the lionsault and had to no-sell the fact I had completely missed him, but it was what it was. The most important thing was that after he went over, the audience was shocked. They didn't chant "Bullshit" like Vince had hoped, but they certainly didn't buy it either, and that's the way he wanted it.

What they did buy was the entertainment value of the campy Fandango character, especially the next night.

Every year, the *Raw* after WrestleMania is notorious for being infested with hardcore fans from around the world who try to highjack the show by doing whatever they want, regardless of the performers' or writers' intentions. They seem to be more concerned with getting themselves over than sitting back and enjoying the show, and it's become an annual tradition to see what ridiculous shit they come up with throughout the course of the night.

So at the *Raw* after WrestleMania 29 at the Izod Center in New Jersey, those wacky hardcore fans made Fandango the most over character in the company. All night long, the crowd sang his theme song, "ChaChaLaLa" (which even made it to number 44 on the UK singles charts), and did the annoying hands up and down dance ad nauseam. When he actually came to the ring they EXPLODED. If you gauged their reaction on the "WWE All-Time Biggest Pop Richter Scale," I would say it landed somewhere between Hulk Hogan in 1986 and The Rock in 2002. (It still wasn't at #RoadWarriorPop levels though.)

Even crazier, when I was leaving the venue after the show, there were literally hundreds of fans in the parking lot singing his song as they were walking to their cars. It was so loud that I called Vince and held the phone out of the window so he could hear it. Say what you want about that character, but at that moment on that night Fandango became a cult hero, and I'm taking some credit for that. Granted, Johnny Curtis had done a great job playing the character and getting himself over, but I laid out the blueprint.

What's the lesson here? It all goes back to the Mike Damone Principle. I had been given an unenviable task, and even though I was furious about it at first, I eventually set my sights on doing the best job I could with the situation I was put in. I did my damnedest to make the Jericho-versus-Fandango match the place to be.

Now, in the long run the Fandango gimmick ended up being just a fad, and a few months later the dancing inferno was put on the back burner. But I'm proud of what Johnny and I were able to accomplish together during those few short weeks, and I'm glad to see that at the time of this writing he's got a good thing going on the WWE main roster, teaming with Tyler Breeze as Breezango.

Even though the Fandango angle has become a private joke between Vince and me (when I won the 2014 Slammy for Extreme Moment of the Year, Vince chose Fandango to accept the trophy in my absence), when I got my Mania check I was surprised to see that it was one of the biggest payoffs I'd ever received. It was more than I got for headlining WrestleMania 18 against Triple H, and the same as what I made for challenging CM Punk for the world championship the year before.

Undertaker's advice was right. I'd made the most of the chance Vince had given me, and he had taken care of me in return . . . handsomely.

THE DAMONE PRINCIPLE applies to rock 'n' roll as well, as I learned when Fozzy was on the Do You Wanna Start a War tour and we were asked to play on the widely popular KISS Kruise, sailing from Miami to Jamaica over the course of four days. All that was required from us was to do three shows, one meet and greet, and I would record a podcast episode of *Talk Is Jericho* with KISS mega manager, the legendary Doc McGhee.

We jumped at the chance. Hell, I would've done a dozen shows for free and swabbed the poop deck with poop if they wanted us to. I mean come on, we would be touring with motherfuckin' KISS!!

We were stoked when we boarded the *Norwegian Pearl* in Miami like the damn rock stars we were. We checked in and were given a packet that listed our schedule for the trip, including the set times for our three shows. I'm always a stickler for details, so I checked to see when we would be playing and more importantly, if we would be "clashing" (aka playing at the same time) with any of the other bands. The first show was free and clear, as we were slated to play as the last band of the night, which was perfect, as everybody was going to be in a partying mood and would be ready to rock. I was right, as the show was jam-packed and the crowd was raucously raucous. The third show was in the middle of the day on the main deck, so I figured we would have a decent crowd, even if it was just rubberneckers having a Mai Tai and hanging out in the sun. Once again, I was right.

But it was the second show's set time that made me shiver me timbers. The gig was the next night at the seemingly prime time of 8 p.m., which under normal circumstances would've made me happy. But that particular time slot scared the shit out of me for one reason: we were playing at the same time as KISS . . . on the KISS Kruise.

Isn't this great?

When I asked the Kruise director (he wasn't as cute as Julie McCoy) why on God's (gave rock 'n' roll to you) green earth they would book a band to play opposite KISS on the KISS Kruise, he explained that the theater they were playing only held fifteen hundred people and there were almost three thousand on the ship. So those who weren't able to get in to see KISS would be ready, willing, and able to rock with Fozzy instead, right?

Wrong. What he didn't tell me was that there were big screens scattered throughout the ship showing a live stream of the KISS concert as they played their classic album *Alive!* in its entirety. Duh! Who in the hell was going to show up to see us play? Maybe not even me, as *Alive!* was one of my favorite albums, and I wasn't sure I wanted to miss that for my own Fozzy show.

But instead of caving in under the crushing disappointment (and slight embarrassment) of playing in front of the 112 people who showed up on the main deck that held about 2,500, we decided to make the best of what we'd been given and make our Fozzy gig THE place to be on that ship at that time.

I didn't care that KISS was hosting us; we wanted all 112 of those people to have the time of their lives and go back home thinking that even though KISS were the kings of the mountain, Fozzy would be the next ones to take the oath.

We went into that show with the attitude that we wanted to give KISS a Destroyer of their own and blow them out of the water, pun intended.

And those few people who chose to spend their night with us were rewarded with a hotter than hell rock show, for sure. We worked that tiny crowd just as hard as if we were rocking them in Madison Square Garden (which was the mindset of KISS themselves in their early club days). It ended up being one of my favorite shows we've done, made even more memorable by the fact it was Halloween night. So there were quite a few rockers in the crowd dressed in costumes, including me wearing Paul Stanley's 1973 Bandit makeup, and another dude dressed up as a toilet. Have you ever seen a commode moshing? It's quite the sight. Thankfully we weren't the shits, as we tried to wipe the floor with KISS (see what I did there?). And when the last song ended, we had gained an additional 112 lifelong Fozzy fans.

Evidently those 112 people wasted no time telling everyone how much fun they had at our show, because when I saw Doc McGhee the next day, he told me, "I heard you guys had a great show last night."

"Really? Where did you hear that? There was hardly anybody there."

"We're on a cruise ship, Chris. Word gets around pretty quickly."

Good point.

The bottom mainline was we had made the best of what we were given that night and the good news traveled fast.

"Wherever you are, that's the place to be," Damone had said, and on that night the place to be was at the Fozzy gig on the KISS Kruise.

Isn't this great?

CHAPTER 2

THE JERICHO PRINCIPLE

BELIEVE IN YOURSELF OR NOBODY ELSE WILL

I just feel I can be anything that I might ever wish to be,
and fantasize just what I want to be,
make my wildest dreams come true . . .
—IRON MAIDEN, "WILDEST DREAMS"

Rock star or pro wrestler?

That was my quandary when I was fourteen years old. Both captured my imagination, and even though I didn't have much of an understanding of what being a rock star or a wrestler entailed, I had a feeling . . . an instinct . . . that I could be good at both. The problem was they seemed as unattainable as the hottest girl in my high school, Roxanne Falk. I had a huge crush on her and at first she wouldn't even give me the time of day. But after months of flirting, wooing, and charming, I'm proud to say

I ended up making out with her on the dance floor at a social once. Yeah, I know I said ONCE . . . but it still counts!

Swapping spit with Roxanne was a great motivator for me, because it showed that with enough hard work and persistence, I could make even the most seemingly impossible dream come true. So after conquering (kind of) Falk Mountain, I set my sights on breaking into wrestling and music. But the only question was, how?

Now, keep in mind that in 1987 there was no Internet where you could learn about wrestling schools or find like-minded musicians to form a band with (thankfully, I found some in high school), so I was pretty much left to my own devices. Recently, I read Arnold Schwarzenegger's autobiography and he told the story of how he decided as an young teenager (about the same age as I was at this time) that he was going to be the greatest bodybuilder ever and the biggest movie star in the world. I'm sure when his buddies in the small town of Thal, Austria, heard about this double fantasy, they gave him the same reaction that my buddies in the small town of Winnipeg, Canada, gave me: mocking disbelief.

I'm sure if I said I wanted to be an astronaut and a pharmacist or the premier of Manitoba and a rodeo clown, my friends probably wouldn't have batted an eye. But to say I had dreams of playing rock 'n' roll AND being a WWE champion made me look like Donald Trump's hair in a windstorm . . . really stupid.

I remember swimming at my friend Scott Shippam's house in the summer of 1989, and after a rousing sing-along of his mantra "Give 'er, give 'er, up Ship's river!" a dude named Pete LeDrew gave his unsolicited opinion about my ambitions.

"You don't really think you're going to make it in wrestling, do you?" he said with a smirk. "I mean, you're way too small."

I stared him in the eye and then pushed his head under the water until he drowned. I spent ten years in jail for manslaughter and the day I got out, I enrolled in the Hart Brothers Pro Wrestling Camp.

Actually, I didn't do a damn thing except tell him that I thought I could make it. But his doubts made me feel self-concious and even worse, hatched a worm of doubt inside my head. And I didn't like that at all.

Pete LeDrew wasn't being malicious, nor was he alone in his opinion about my chances for success. It's just that my dreams seemed so far-fetched to the people that knew just plain old Chris Irvine; and I heard variations of Pete's presumptions multiple times that summer. It seemed like everyone I knew felt I didn't have the size to make it in wrestling, nor the talent to get into music. Everybody that is, but me. Those negative Neegans were making it sound like I should smash my head in with a barbed-wire bat for having the audacity to believe in myself, but I didn't care. I was too busy reaching out to wrestling schools and writing songs to give a fuck.

You see, I NEVER thought I was too small or not talented enough to do what I wanted to do, and I didn't appreciate anybody who felt differently. The way I saw it, you were either with me or against me in my quest for fire, and if you were against me, well, you were a muttonhead and I really didn't have any use for you anyway.

I told the story in my first book (the wildly popular *New York Times* bestseller *A Lion's Tale*) about having a whole church full of people laugh at me when my pastor told them I was moving from Winnipeg to Calgary to pursue my dream of becoming a wrestler. That incident scarred me, and I never returned to that church again. (Bitter Author's note: I've been back to Winnipeg dozens of times over the last twenty-six years, but I still haven't stepped one foot into that place. I guess it's always going to have negative connotations for me.)

Once I got out of Winnipeg and moved to Calgary to start training, things changed. I found once I stopped talking about getting into wrestling and actually started doing it, the haters and skaters dwindled. That was another lesson learned that could almost be its own principle: stop talking about doing things and actually start doing them.

My belief in myself has never wavered, except that is for the times I've been stricken by The Jericho Curse. If you're not familiar with that, well, you should go back and read my three previous *New York Times* bestselling books, Junior!

Long story short, throughout my wrestling career, whenever I started with a new company I always got off on the wrong foot. Whether it was in Mexico, Japan, Germany, ECW, WCW, or WWE, it always seemed that my first appearance in the company was a disaster. That's probably why I've wrestled exclusively for the WWE for the last seventeen years. I'm too scared to go anywhere else!

But despite debuting in every new promotion on an all-time low, I refused to let the disheartening debuts crack the core of who I knew I was inside. It sucked to stink out the joint whenever I first appeared fresh-faced and untested in a new company, but deep down I always knew I would get over it and make it to the next level.

After my first weekend in ECW, when Paul Heyman mysteriously "lost" the tapes of my first-ever ECW TV match against Rob Van Dam, I had a sneaking suspicion that those tapes were actually fine and el dandy, but Paul didn't want to air the match because it sucked. I never asked, but it was nearly enough to crush my ego. I mean, it had taken almost ONE YEAR to get booked in ECW, and the first TV match I had was so bad it was erased from existence? That's not good.

But I knew that I would do better, so I held my head high and promised myself the next time would be different. And it was, as the next weekend I tore the house down with Mick Foley in Queens and again the next night against Taz in the ECW Arena. It had taken me a minute, but I regained my stuck mojo pretty damn quickly . . . albeit after letting myself and my peers down first. Unfortunately for me, the Curse bit me in the ass again when I started a new company a few months later.

After my first WCW match with Mr. J.L. at a TV taping in Dalton, Georgia, booker Terry Taylor walked past me and snorted with disgust. "Are you sure you have any clue what the hell you're doing?"

Wow, nice confidence builder. I was nervous enough already, and that little quip almost killed me right there. It sucks to have a stinker (or an "abortion" as we call it in the biz) and get chewed out by the booker, but it's even worse to have to come back to the dressing room and face your fellow performers.

When I walked back into the locker room, most of the guys suddenly found something very interesting about the toes of their boots, and kept their heads to the floor. I guess it was either that or look me in the eye and laugh, as they were so embarrassed for me. Thankfully, Eddie Guerrero pulled me aside and gave me a pep talk.

"I know that wasn't the real you. You're nervous, and as a result you didn't look very good out there. I've seen you work, I know you can do better. Next match, just take your time and be Chris Jericho. That will be more than enough to get over with the fans and to impress everybody here."

His words stuck with me during my next match with journeyman wrestler The Gambler, and with the help of his advice, we had a good match and the Curse was vanquished once again. Thanks, Eddie.

By not panicking and following my instincts, I proved to Terry Taylor and everyone else in WCW that I did in fact have a clue what the hell I was doing.

But that wasn't the end of the Curse. After my mediocre first match with The Rock on *Monday Night Raw*, Jeff Jarrett asked me how I thought it went. That's the telltale sign in wrestling that the person asking the question thought your match was the shits of the drizzling variety. I knew the match wasn't good, but when Jeff asked, I replied, "It wasn't bad, but it will be better next time." It was the first thing that came into my mind and it was the truth. Once again I knew I could do better, although it's up for debate how many others in the WWE locker room circa 1999 agreed with me. But it didn't take long for them to change their minds. Once I got my wings and figured out how to adapt to the WWE way of doing things, I had great matches with almost all of them, including The Rock. He became one of my favorite opponents and we headlined multiple PPVs together, exchanged the world title a few times, and even had what he claims to be his favorite match ever at a live event in Honolulu, Hawaii.

Even though I started performing up to my potential and earned the respect of my peers, I still wasn't immune to the odd abortion here and there, including a match against Raven on *Raw* a few years later. It was one of those nights, and even though we'd had great matches in the past, that time it just didn't click and was embarrassingly bad.

In the early 2000s, they would set up a TV in catering and air *Raw* the next day before the *Smackdown* tapings. I was hanging in the back of the room when the Raven match came on, and I'll never forget Steve Austin laughing in disbelief and throwing his baseball cap against the wall in protest of how rotten it was. If I could've pulled the TV plug out of the wall, summoned a battalion of skeleton zombies to attack the arena Evil Dead 2 style, and opened the earth to swallow the place whole, I would have. But alas, I was just a mere mortal (and the proprietor of a crappy match) and was forced to deal with the roasting like a real man. So I did the most honorable thing a real man could do: snuck out the back door with my lion's tale between my legs before anybody spotted me.

I skulked down the hall with the braying of Austin's guffaws still ringing in my ears, and remembered something that Vince McMahon told me when I first came to the WWE: "Nobody bats a thousand, Chris."

That statement made perfect sense and was similar to what the great Mexican *luchador* Negro Casas told me after I majorly screwed up the finish of our main-event match one night. "You can't change today. You can only learn and change tomorrow." Sage advice indeed.

You can't always hit a home run, but when you strike out, remember the times you did nail it out of the park and let the confidence of that experience buoy your mentality. I haven't always made the right decision or done the right thing, but I gave it my all every time, and never stopped believing in myself.

Although to this day, if I listen really hard on a cold windy night, I can still hear the howls of Stone Cold Steve Austin booming inside my head.

CHAPTER 3

THE KEITH RICHARDS PRINCIPLE

FIND A WAY TO MAKE IT WORK

Making it work takes a little longer,
making it work takes a little time . . .
—DOUG AND THE SLUGS, "MAKING IT WORK"

I really don't like it when I ask someone to go somewhere and they say something like "Ummm, I'd like to go but I have to work tomorrow" or "I want to go but I don't have a friend to go with."

Blah blah blah.

If you don't WANT to go that's fine, but if it's something you really want to do then don't give me any excuses. Have to work in the morning? Then drink an extra cup of coffee if you're tired. Don't have somebody to go with? Go solo and make friends.

It's easy to think of a hundred reasons why something won't work, but I'd rather find the reasons to MAKE it work. If you want your dreams to come true, stop thinking of excuses and start making realities. This is the way I've always lived my life, and that credo remains my golden rule to this day.

When Fozzy was offered the chance to support Motörhead in 2005 at their thirtieth anniversary show in Los Angeles, it was too good of an opportunity to pass up. It was a huge chance for us to play with one of the most legendary bands in rock 'n' roll history, and just being on the same bill with them would put us on a different level.

The problem was we weren't touring at the time, and it wasn't exactly an easy trip to Los Angeles for an Atlanta-based band. It's expensive to fly to the other side of the country for a one-off show, and there were a dozen reasons why we should have declined the offer. But there was one simple reason to say the heck with it and find a way to make it work: we wanted to do the gig.

So we did it.

We pooled our resources and frequent flyer miles, called our West Coast endorsers to set us up with gear so we wouldn't have to pay any shipping costs, took care of the financial details, and the next thing you know, we were rocking the stage as the opening band for fucking Motörhead!

Now, I can't say that we tore the house down with the fans (most of them stood staring at us like we had cocks for noses), but we created a relationship with Motörhead and left a good impression on them. So much so that guitarist Phil Campbell played with us onstage at the Whiskey a Go Go in LA and the Bloodstock festival in England, and even played the solo for "She's My Addiction" on the *Sin and Bones* album, at his request.

Lemmy saw our set that night and liked our "good fuckin energy," which started a friendship between him and me that lasted until the day he died. So many great things happened as a result of us going out of our way to play that show, even though it would've been way easier to just stay home and save the money. But we found a way to make it work, and we were glad we did.

One of my favorite movies is the original *Dawn of the Dead* (the remake is pretty badass too), and there's a great scene towards the end when Ken Foree's Peter is trapped on the top floor of a building, surrounded by zombies. Even though a chopper awaits to take him to safety on the roof above, he's tired of fighting and doesn't have it in him to get through the maze of the undead. Broken, beat, and scarred, he puts his revolver up to his forehead, but before he can muster up the will to pull the trigger, he sees a clear path through the mass of walkers, shakes himself out of his suicide pity party, and makes a run for it. He fights his way through the pack, races up a ladder to the roof, and climbs in the chopper to safety just as it takes off!

That scene is the perfect example of what I'm preaching to you today, Constant Reader. Peter could've just rolled into a ball and waited to get eaten alive by the flesh-chomping zombies, but instead he beat the odds and survived. There's a lesson there: it may not be easy, but you can always find a way to make it work. Even if we're talking about the struggles we face every day, it's worth it to battle through the zombies to get what you want.

"Battle through the zombies" actually sounds pretty kooky. Can we get that trending worldwide on Twitter please? Please put this book down and go post #battlethroughthezombies NOW and tag @iamjericho while you're at it.

While I'm waiting, I'll just hum my favorite Van Damme Substitution song. What's a "Van Damme Substitution" song you ask? Well, I'll tell you . . . because that's the start of the story of how I was able to #battlethroughthezombies to meet Keith Richards.

Back in 1990 when I first moved to Okotoks, Canada, to train with the Hart brothers, I didn't have a pot to piss in, nor the piss to fill it. So when I was invited to live with Bev and Jerry Palko in exchange for painting the fence surrounding their massive farm, it was a godsend. They were amazing people and I wouldn't be where I am today without them.

Their son Tyler and I became great friends (still are) and we spent a lot of time hanging out listening to music and watching TV. That led to us becoming slightly obsessed with two things: the dancing skills of MC Hammer (and his hype man, No Bones) and the acting skills of Jean Claude Van Damme. A strange combination to be sure, which got stranger when we decided to combine the two '90s pop culture icons.

"U Can't Touch This" was the biggest song in the country at the time, and we thought it would be funny if we replaced the chorus with JCVD's name. Which made it go a little something like this:

> Da da dah
> Da da da-dah
> Claude Van Damme
> Da da dah
> Da da da-dah
> Claude Van Damme . . .

Rinse, wash, repeat.

Kind of stupid for sure, but it made us laugh every time. Even more ridiculous was that in order to make his name fit within the meter of the song, we had to leave "Jean" off and just sing "Claude Van Damme." We had so much fun with it that it wasn't long before the Van Damme Substitution game mutated its way into every song we heard, because it was so easy to insert the name into any chorus.

Hey, Mr. DJ, let's give a few examples . . . please cue up some ZZ Top:

> The girls come running just as fast as they can,
> Cause every girl's crazy about Claude Van Damme . . .

Okay, now how about a little "Der Kommissar" by Falco?

Jean Claude Van Damme
Uh oh oh
Claude Van Damme is in town
Uh oh oh . . .

You get the point. Not only did the VDS remixes make us laugh, but I was sure if we sang them with commitment they would make other people laugh too. For years, I hummed "U Can't Touch This" with the Van Damme chorus, but never had a forum to share the joke . . . until Jimmy Fallon got his own late-night talk show. I loved his work on *Saturday Night Live*, knew he would get my humor, and vowed if I were ever invited on as a guest, I'd pitch the idea.

I finally did get invited onto *Late Night with Jimmy Fallon* a few years later in 2010, but I backed off with the VDS suggestion because it was my first time on, and I thought it would be out of line to pitch such a weird idea. But the segment went well, and when I was invited back in 2012, I called Jimmy's producer, Jim Juvonen, and explained the idea.

He asked if I could send him a sample, so I warbled a medley of VDS tunes into my voice app and shot the file over. He emailed me back and said he liked it and would pitch the idea to Jimmy. Then a few days later, he let me know that while they liked the idea, they had decided against using it. I was bummed, but you can't fight city hall, and I figured that was that.

A few nights later, I was getting ready in my dressing room twenty minutes before the start of the show, when Jimmy, a great guy with infectious energy, exploded into the room like a whirling dervish.

"Chris, great to see you! Thanks for coming back on the show. Listen, I just heard about your Van Damme idea and I love it! It's hilarious and I'd like to do it!"

Wow, that was a pleasant surprise, but it made me a little nervous. Obviously, I loved the idea too, but we hadn't rehearsed anything and this was literally the last minute. How would we be able to pull it off on the spot? I expressed my concern to the boss.

"Don't worry about it, man. Quest will just follow along with you."

Questlove is the leader of Jimmy's house band, the Roots, and they are the best in the world at what they do. They can play anything, and after I thought about it, I realized they'd have no problem improving the whole bit. We would find a way to make it work.

My segment started, and after about five minutes in, Jimmy asked me about the Van Damme Substitution song. I smiled and bashfully asked the audience if they'd like to hear a sample. Of course they applauded, as the prospect of seeing this Chris Jericho wrestler guy singing songs about Jean Claude Van Damme was obviously too good to ignore.

I had given Quest a setlist of the songs for the medley, so we started off strong with "U Can't Touch This," leading right into "Sharp Dressed Man" (complete with a weird shimmy and shake across the stage), and finished off with "Der Kommissar." The crowd burst into legit applause at the absurdity of what they were seeing, and the Roots were spot-on with their timing throughout the segment. But the best part of the whole bit was when Jimmy (who had been laughing his ass off and totally putting me over like a true pro) surprised me with a VDS of his own. He busted out "Hunger Strike" by Temple of the Dog, and changed the chorus accordingly. Maestro, please cue up some Dog.

(Jimmy doing the Eddie Vedder part)—Jean Claude Van Damme
(Me doing the high Chris Cornell part)—Jean Claude Van
    Dammmm-hahammmm
(Jimmy)—Jean Claude Van Damme
(Me)—Jean Claude Van Dammmm-hahammmm . . .

I'd never sung the tune before, but I went for it and nailed that mofo. It was a great end to a great bit, and definitely one of the funniest things I've been involved with on national TV.

So what does this have to do with meeting Keith Richards? Hold your wild horses, I'm getting to that.

About a year and a half later, I was invited back on *Fallon* to talk about my match with Fandango at WrestleMania 29, which happened to be taking place just nine miles away at MetLife Stadium in New Jersey.

A few days before the show, Jim Juvonen called me to ask if I wanted to do another VDS spot. Does the Pope shit in the woods? Of course I wanted to!

I told him I'd think of a new theme, and a few hours later I hummed another medley into my iPhone, this time using boy bands as my inspiration.

Maestro, please cue up a little New Kids on the Block, "The Right Stuff."

Oh Oh Oooooh Ooooh
Oh Oh OooooOh
Oh Oh Oooooh Oooh,
Claude Van Damme.

Then a little Backstreet Boys, please:

Tell me why, ain't nothing but a heartache
Tell me why, ain't nothing but a mistake
Tell me why, I never wanna hear you say
I want Claude Van Damme . . .

Now, let's bring it back around with a little modern twist and play some One Direction:

Baby, you light up my world like nobody else
The way you flip your hair gets me overwhelmed,

But when you smile at the ground it ain't hard to tell,
Oh Oh Oh
You don't know Jean Claude Van Damme,
Oh Oh Oh
You don't know Jean Claude Van Damme!

This time the bit was approved and when I arrived at 30 Rock, I went straight into rehearsal and worked it out with the Roots. The medley killed for the second time in a row, and Jimmy once again put me over by singing along, especially on the 1D tune.

Now, I'm sure you have been wildly entertained by my VDS story, but I know you've been waiting patiently to hear my hanging out with Keith Richards story, right? Okay, allow me to come to your emotional rescue and tell you.

I was sitting in producer Jim's office after my rehearsal with the Roots, shooting the breeze and catching up. The subject turned to upcoming shows, and Jim pointed out a calendar on the wall with the next few weeks of guests scrawled under each date. It was a Thursday, and when I looked to see who was going to be there the following week, I was impressed that Keith Richards was scheduled for Monday.

Apparently, out of all the American talk shows, Keith only did Jimmy's and had made multiple appearances, smashing it every time.

"If you're going to be in town, you should come by. I'm sure Jimmy will introduce you."

I thanked him for the offer, but told him since *Raw* was on Monday, I wouldn't be able to make it.

Or would I?

Meeting Keith Richards had been a dream of mine for years, as I'd been a marginal Stones fan since I was a kid. But ironically enough, it wasn't until I saw their reunion concert in December of 2012 on PPV—promoted by Vincent K. McMahon himself—that I got REALLY into them. Now that the Stones were one of my all-time favorites, I started thinking about the logistics of whether I might actually be able to make this meeting happen. *Raw* was nine miles away at the Izod Center in New Jersey, and under normal circumstances that wouldn't have presented a problem. But Jimmy taped his show at 5:30 p.m., which meant the show wouldn't be over till around 6:30 p.m., which meant I wouldn't get of there until around 7 p.m. That would still give me an hour to get to *Raw* before it started at 8 p.m., but nine miles in New York City at rush hour could take nine hours. However, this was a once in a lifetime chance, so I decided I needed to find a way to make it work. This was a chance I had to take . . . after all, how many chances was I going to get to meet Keith fuckin' Richards, right?

When Jimmy came into my dressing room before the show, I mentioned what his producer had told me about Keef.

"Dude, he's like the nicest guy ever. If you come down here, I promise I'll introduce you to him. He'll be happy to meet you!"

It sounded too good to be true, so I was very direct with my retort.

"Jimmy, are you just stroking me? Is this like a Hollywood thing where you're saying it but not meaning it? Because if you're serious, I'm telling you right now I'll be here on Monday."

"Be here Monday at 5 p.m. sharp and I'll introduce you to him. No bullshit. I'll make it happen."

Well, once he said that, there was no way that I wasn't going to take him up on it. But how was it going to work? There were still a dozen things that could go wrong to cause me to be late for *Raw*, or even miss it completely. It would have been a lot easier to thank him for the offer and try to catch Keith the next time he was in town. But I knew there might not be a next time, so I had to find a way to make it happen now.

The first step was to hire a car to take me into the city. If I didn't have to worry about parking, that would save me some serious time. I could get dropped off directly at 30 Rock and have the car wait until I was done, then have it take me back to Jersey pronto. If traffic wasn't too bad and I was able to connect with

Keef directly after the show, I could be back at the arena by 7:45 p.m. Which would be great, unless I was in the first segment of *Raw* at 8 p.m. sharp, in which case I'd be cutting it way too close.

So the next step was to try and see if my segment could be placed later in the show. It was the day after my big loss to Fandango at Mania, so I was scheduled to rush the ring as he cut a promo and give him a beatdown. There wasn't much to rehearse, which helped my cause, so I tracked down Dave Kapoor and told him about my plan to see if he could help.

"That's up to Vince, but I'll do the best I can to have it put it on later."

I knew Dave would do what he could, but he wasn't the boss, and even though my original strategy was to kayfabe Vince about my journey into the city, I knew the smarter move was to keep him in the loop. That way if something went wrong, at least he would know about it. But there was a much bigger potential problem: what if he said no?

That was a chance I was willing to take, but if he forbade me from going and I had to decide between the WWE and Keef, I honestly wasn't sure which one I'd choose. The good news was that since the Stones were Vince's favorite band not named AC/DC (he had seen them live, hired a Stones cover band to play a WrestleMania after-party, and had promoted their reunion concert a few months earlier), I figured if anybody would understand my desire to meet Keith, it would be him.

I found him in his office and explained that I had the chance to meet Keith in the city, but might not be back to the arena until close to showtime.

"I know you understand how rare of an opportunity this is, and I really want to do it. It would really help me if you could put me as late in the show as possible. I really think I can make it back in time."

Vince looked at me with a reflective gaze. "I've never met any of the Stones," he mused. "I was supposed to before the PPV we did together, but traffic was bad and I missed my shot."

Then he stared at me sternly.

"Well, Chris, you have to go. I'll try to put you on later in the show, but don't fuck me on this. You better have plan A, B, and C to get back here on time."

"I'll rent a helicopter to get me here if I have to, Vince. I won't miss *Raw*, I promise."

We shook hands as he told me have a good time and that was that. It reminded me of the time I asked my mom if I could sleep over at my friend Gouge's house when I was sixteen years old, knowing that he was having a party and we were going to be drinking. When she said yes, I felt like I had just escaped from jail, and I was feeling that same euphoria of freedom (sounds like an album title) right now. However, as cool as drinking with the Gouge was, I had a feeling that hanging out with Keef was gonna be a whole lot cooler.

The SUV showed up at the arena at 4 p.m. sharp, and I was off to the city. Traffic was pretty light and I arrived at 4:30, a full thirty minutes early, so I picked up my credentials from security and went up the elevator to Fallon's greenroom at the end of the hall.

I walked in and was surprised to see Dennis Rodman sitting on the plush green couch, surrounded by his entourage. I hadn't seen Dennis in fifteen years, since we were both working in WCW. He was a hot commodity at the time, and Eric Bischoff had signed him for a handful of PPVs that had drawn some pretty big numbers. (Even the one where he arrived an hour before the show and fell asleep in his corner holding the tag rope DURING his match.)

But overall Dennis was a good guy, and it was nice to see him again. We shot the breeze for a few minutes, and he told the story of how he had recently been with Kim Jong-un in North Korea and had attempted to facilitate world peace by arranging a phone call between Kim and President Obama. However, the tale was cut short when Jimmy (ever the ball of energy) popped his head into the room and said, "Hey, Dennis! Great to see you, man! Chris, are you all set?"

I nodded and followed Jimmy out the door. The fact that he hadn't invited one of the top-ten most famous players in NBA history to join us showed just how exclusive this meeting really was.

"Keith just arrived and he's in a great mood. I know you've got to get out of here, so let's go see him now before he gets busy."

I was amazed by Jimmy's hospitality and how concerned he was with my situation, despite the fact that he had his own national talk show to prepare for. But none of that mattered as we rounded the corner and stopped at a closed door. Jimmy knocked twice and a middle-aged lady opened it and let us inside. We walked into the small sixteen-by-sixteen-foot room, and there was Keith Richards, one of the biggest rock stars of all time standing in the corner. He was a few inches shorter than me, with a gray headband wrapped around his tousled gray hair, smoking a gray cigarette. The wrinkles on his face were more prominent in person and there was a slight old-man's pot belly discernable beneath his T-shirt (also gray) that displayed the slogan I ONLY TAKE THE STUFF TO STOP THE BLEEDIN' emblazoned across the front.

He smiled and cackled his famous gargling razor laugh.

"Jimmy! How are you, man?"

"I didn't think you were in here, Keith. I couldn't smell any cigarette smoke," Jimmy remarked with a smile.

"Yeah, man, I just got this new ashtray that sucks up the smoke so you can't smell it," he said with wonder, despite the fact that my grandma had the same contraption in 1977.

"Keith, this is my friend Chris Jericho. He's with the WWE and just wrestled in MetLife stadium yesterday in front of seventy thousand people!"

Keef took a drag of his smoke and slurred, "Far out, man," with a nod. I'm sure he was thinking, Wow, you played one stadium? Congrats, kid, that's a good little accomplishment for you . . . now get back to me when you've played a thousand of 'em like I have.

I nervously mumbled a few words about how much of an honor it was to meet him, then recovered quickly and asked him about his grapefruits. Now, I wasn't referring to Vince McMahon testicular grapefruits, but rather the special strain of large citrus plants he grew at his home that Jimmy had told me about earlier. Keith launched excitedly into a detailed description of his special produce and how he cultivated them. Then he reached into the mini-fridge on the floor and pulled out a glass bottle for Jimmy.

"This is the soda from Jamaica I was telling you about, man. I brought you a sample. You're going to love it."

After more small talk, I mentioned that I'd seen the Stones PPV a few months earlier and one song in particular had stood out to me. They had done a smoking rendition of Freddie King's "Going Down," featuring a high-powered four-man guitar duel between Gary Clark Jr., John Mayer, Ronnie Wood, and Keith himself. I mentioned that while the other three guys had pulled out their most dexterous solos, when it was Keith's turn he merely played one note, bent up the string and struck a kickass pose. Then he swaggered back to the drums like a fuckin' boss with a shit-eating grin. It was the coolest thing I'd ever seen, and I asked him about it.

"Well, everybody was playing so busy, I decided to just pick one note and stick with it. But I had to make sure it was a good one!" he quipped before barking another barrage of his boisterous laugh.

I joined in and mentioned how cool it was to see the Stones back on stage after a lengthy layoff, and asked if they were thinking about doing any more shows.

"Absolutely! I knew if I could just convince HIM to play one show, that HE would get the bug again and HE would want to do more, and that's what happened. HE was on the phone with me the next day to talk about a tour."

I realized of course that the HE and HIM to whom Keith was referring was Mick Jagger, who'd famously feuded with his pal over the past few years. But now that the heat had apparently blown over, I'd just been given the exclusive news by one of the Glimmer Twins that the Rolling Stones were ready to do some more dirty work, baby!

We chatted for a few more minutes as Jimmy explained what they had planned for that evening, including a bit where Keef would be sitting in the audience heckling himself as he got interviewed ("Whatever you want, Jimmy, anything for you, man"). Then Jimmy asked if he could take a picture of me with Jumpin' Jack Flash himself.

"Of course, man! Just make sure you get my good side," Richards said with a grin. "Wait a second, I'm sixty-nine years old . . . I don't have a good side!" (Insert rusty-blade chuckle here.)

He slid his arm around me and I laughed as Jimmy snapped the photo. It was a great shot and I've gotten more comments about that picture than any other I've taken. As a matter of fact, when I sent it to Guns N' Roses guitarist and my bro Slash, he dug it so much that he said he was going to print it out and save it.

Keith then told his assistant to give me one of the exclusive Keef T-shirts they had brought with them, stacked in small pile in the corner.

"What size are you, man?" he asked. When I told him large would be fine, he said, "Take a medium too, just in case. Give the one that doesn't fit to your grandma . . . she'll know who I am!" He cackled once again.

We thanked him for his hospitality, and I shook his hand and proclaimed my eternal respect for him and his band as we left the room.

Jimmy and I stood in the hallway for a few moments like excited groupies, buzzing about the previous fifteen minutes. I couldn't thank him enough for arranging the once in a lifetime meeting and he said, "I told you I would make it happen!"

Then he clapped me on the back and said he had to go to work, which was perfect timing, because I did too. The best part was that it was only 5:15 p.m., which gave me plenty of time to get back to the Izod Center. I even had time to give my regards to Rodman, who was still in the greenroom recounting his tales of Jong-un to anyone who would listen. A few minutes later I was in the SUV, and thanks to the miracle of no traffic was back at the arena about thirty minutes later, at 6:15 p.m. During the drive, I sent the picture of me and Keef to a bunch of my friends, including Vince.

"Awesome," was his one-word response.

When I got back to the Izod Center, I checked out the evening's rundown taped to the wall and was relieved to see my segment was scheduled at the top of the third hour, which would be around 10 p.m. Vince had lived up to his promise and put me on as late as he could, and I in turn had lived up to my promise and gotten back to the arena with plenty of time to spare.

So despite all the reasons why it might not have worked out, I had taken a chance, beat the odds, and met Keith Richards.

A few weeks later, I sent a rare Rolling Stones vinyl box set to Fallon's office as a token of my appreciation. I received a nice email back from him saying what a great time it was and that I had an open invite to return to his show whenever I wanted.

Well, I haven't been invited back since he took over hosting *The Tonight Show*, but when I am, I have a wicked Van Halen/VDS medley that needs to be heard to be believed.

I've got it bad
I've got it bad
I've got it bad
I'm hot for Van Damme . . .

CHAPTER 4

THE VINCE MCMAHON PRINCIPLE

WORK HARD . . . THEN WORK HARDER!

You got me workin', workin' day and night,
And I'll be workin' from sun up to midnight . . .
—MICHAEL JACKSON, "WORKIN' DAY AND NIGHT"

I do a lot of stuff.

Between my WWE career, Fozzy tours, twice weekly episodes of *Talk Is Jericho,* running the Jericho Network, hosting shows, planning cruises, and writing books, it's fair to say that I am at work more than most people. I've been fortunate to turn my various passions into professions because I like being creative, but the bottom line is I like working. It's fun to accept a challenge and then use my brainpower to make it successful. I've always had a strong work ethic, instilled in me at a young age by my parents, and cultivated to the highest degree for the last seventeen years by my WWE boss, Vince McMahon.

As the head of a billion-dollar company that thanks to him has become a worldwide phenomenon, Vince hasn't shirked any responsibilities along the way. Even today, as he approaches his mid-seventies, I get the sense that he works just as hard now as he ever did. His joie de vivre for what he does is infectious, and I honestly enjoy being around him. He's constantly pushing his own boundaries and has no fear of leaving his comfort zone to try new things and expand his business in various ways. They don't always work . . . (cough, XFL, cough) . . . but most of them do, like the WWE Network and last year's *Raw/Smackdown* brand extension, and he continues to expand his business model every year. He also has a motto that I apply to myself when I'm working on all my various business ventures.

"There's no job too big or too small, Chris," he told me one day in his office, as he bent over to pick up and throw away a random bit of trash. It struck me that the head of a billion-dollar company was perfectly happy taking a turn doing janitorial work, because it needed to be done.

His other motto is "I'd never ask you to do something that I wouldn't do myself," which is why you've seen him fall off the sides of cages, have Porta-Pottys of poop poured on him, and even dance and sing in the music video for his song "Stand Back." (Haven't seen it? Please go to YouTube and treat yourself now!) The guy is fearless and willing to try anything if he thinks there's a chance it will benefit his company. This is an attitude I've adopted in my own life, and I promise it will benefit you in your own future endeavors as well.

A few years ago, I hosted the revamped *WWE Tough Enough* on the USA Network. While it wasn't a hit, it was an amazing experience because as the host, I was expected to sit in on the production meetings led by Vince and give my opinions to better the show. Some of my ideas worked, some didn't, but more importantly, Vince taught me how to conduct myself in a professional meeting. Once after I obnoxiously cut somebody off, he took me aside and explained that I didn't always have to be the loudest guy in the room.

"Sometimes it's better just to sit back and survey the situation. If you choose your words carefully, people will pay more attention to what you don't say than what you do. And then when you talk, your words will mean more."

That was something that my friend Chris Benoit was great at: listening. He didn't say much, but when he did, he commanded your complete attention. If he was bothering to talk, you knew he had put great thought into what he was about to say.

After a live episode of *Tough Enough*, I was invited to ride on the WWE corporate jet, so I could make it to the NBC Upfront convention in New York City to do press the next morning. Despite the fact Vince ribbed me and left the TV studio without me, I still made it to the airfield on time, and took a seat on the plane directly facing him. Over the course of the next three hours, we had a blast talking about AC/DC and the Rolling Stones, *Dancing with the Stars* (Vince was very supportive of my decision to do the program and admired the "balls" I had to actually go through with it), old-time wrestling, and ribbing The Big Show, all the while enjoying a few cocktails as two gentlemen are wont to do. As a result, I was pretty loaded when we finally landed in New York around 4 a.m. I was tired and dreading the fact that I was going to have to wake up in a few short hours to get ready for the big press day, but apparently Mr. McMahon didn't feel the same way.

"What are you doing now?" he quizzed me. "Wanna go to the gym and work out?"

"Go to the gym? Are you nuts? I'm wasted and I have to get up in three hours!" I slurred in disbelief.

"So? I have to get up in two."

Needless to say, I didn't accept Vince's offer and went to the hotel to get some much needed sleep. I woke up to a text from my sixty-nine-year old boss sent while he was working out at 4:30 a.m., burying me for not keeping up with him. Meanwhile, I was drooling all over my pillow in a drunken snooze and was barely able to get out of bed.

McMahon: 1
Jericho: 0

When you think about it, Vince's legendary work ethic has transferred to his most successful employees as if by osmosis. Working for him inspires those of us who want to do great things in the WWE and beyond. You don't have to go far to see why Vince's employees who have been successful in other areas have ended up that way.

Look at The Rock, for example. At this point, he's one of the biggest movie stars on the planet, with new movies being shot constantly, a hit HBO television series in *Ballers*, a successful production company producing hit after hit, and all the while maintaining an intense physical regimen. Plus, he's renowned for having a good attitude, a strong work ethic, and being very easy to work with. That comes from Vince as well, as there's no place for prima donnas in his modern-day WWE system. You're expected to do your job to the utmost of your abilities and go the extra mile without question.

John Cena is another example of the McMahon work ethic personified. He was tireless in his efforts for the WWE, inside of the ring and out, including being the most requested Make-A-Wish celebrity or sports figure EVER. Think about that . . . more kids have requested to meet him than anybody else on the planet!

He's also worked his ass off to make a splash in Hollywood and has become one of the most promising comedic actors in the business. Add in a regular guest hosting gig with the *Today* show and a plethora of other projects, and you see how his work ethic is paying off. Hell, the guy even learned how to speak Mandarin Chinese in order to help break the WWE in China. Think about how much of an effort that must've taken . . . I can barely speak English these days!

Dave Bautista also fits in this category after becoming one of the biggest (literally) character actors in the world, and if you don't believe it, find me another guy whose movies have grossed over three million dollars in box office receipts in just a few years.

Big Dave is in the Big Time now.

I also take great pride in also being one of "Vince's guys" when it comes to my business acumen. I don't take every project I'm offered, but I'm not afraid to try new things and take a chance if an opportunity interests me. I'll also do whatever I have to do to make something happen if I think it's a smart move careerwise.

When Fozzy was offered a short tour with Slash and his solo band, the Conspirators, by Slash himself, I knew we had to make it work no matter what. The only issue was there wasn't a lot of money offered, but there comes a time when you have to do things for the Big Picture, not short-term financial reasons.

In this case, the prospect of touring with Slash would not only put us in front of big crowds in the States, but also give us the chance to impress one of the greatest guitar players in history, who would be touring (and needing opening acts) for years to come. Plus, the low-money offer forced us to get crafty with the budget. Fozzy's manager, Mark Willis, and I challenged each other to make the tour happen and to make it profitable. It wasn't easy, but we did it.

We made a few concessions, like downgrading from a tour bus to a van and going out with only two crew members, but we doubled our VIP efforts, built up our merchandise, and booked a few headlining shows on the days off in between Slash gigs. We also used our "in case of emergency" endorsement money from the amazing people at Monster Energy (shout-out to Matt Larsen) that we had saved for a rainy-day tour like this. When it was all sang and done, after playing five awesome shows with Slash and two headlining gigs of our own, Rich Ward (Fozzy's guitar player and my partner in crime) and I were able to pay all our expenses and still walk away with a profit. More importantly, we earned Slash's respect, as he told us that we were the best opening band he'd had on the tour so far, and high praise like that can't be bought. So even though it required a lot of planning, scrimping, and extra work to make those shows happen, it paid off big time.

The point I'm trying to get across is if something is worth doing, then you need to put in the effort to make it work. And that motto is the secret behind the success of my podcast, *Talk Is Jericho*.

After finishing up a two-year run of *The Rock of Jericho* show on Nikki Sixx's Sixx Sense channel on SiriusXM, I was looking for another radio gig. I really enjoyed the weekly interview segments on *Rock of Jericho* with my various musician friends and wanted to continue the chat-show format but wasn't sure how.

Then like a stunner out of nowhere, I got a call from Steve Austin (who had recently started his own podcast), asking me if I'd be interested in doing one of my own.

I was excited at the prospect and thought it would be the perfect forum for me to continue to hone the interviewing skills I'd been working on since I'd studied journalism at Red River College in Winnipeg (represent, yo!), twenty-five years prior.

Steve hooked me up with his boss, Norm Pattiz, who had created an audio kingdom with the Westwood One radio network back in the 1970s. He had since founded the PodcastOne network, after having the foresight to see that podcasts were the future of radio.

Norm was a charismatic guy, funny and driven, who reminded me a lot of Vince McMahon. They both had the bravado, fearlessness, and implied arrogance that went along with being the head of a self-created multimillion-dollar pop culture empire. I'd experienced Lorne Michaels to be the same way when I worked for him on *MacGruber*. (Check out the hilarious summit between the two of us in my humorous handbook, *The Best in the World*.)

Norm and I hit it off immediately, and we decided to work together only a few minutes after we met. The best part of starting *Talk Is Jericho* for me was that I was going to get a hundred percent creative control over the content of the podcast, which was important because my mission was to make *TIJ* more than just a wrestling show. I wanted it to reflect the diverse interests of Chris Jericho. Wrestling would be a part of it for sure, but I also wanted to have musicians, paranormal experts, comedians, porn stars, athletes, family, friends, and anything in between on as well. Basically, anybody who I felt was interesting enough to carry on a conversation with me for an hour could make the cut. I wanted *Talk Is Jericho* to be like *The Tonight Show* in that people tuned in because they liked Jimmy Fallon, not because of any particular guest.

So that's how I structured it.

Austin was my first guest and Edge was my second, but within the next ten episodes, I had Eddie Trunk on to talk about KISS in the Hall of Fame, M. Shadows to talk video games, Ted Irvine to talk old-time hockey, and a ghost hunter to talk elephants. Actually, the ghost hunter spoke about ghosts, but you get the idea.

The wrestling guests got the most downloads, but my non-wrestling shows drew some great numbers right off the bat as well. As a result, *Talk Is Jericho* was an instant hit.

I was ecstatic, but my mission was to keep it a hit and also expand my audience. I felt from the start that my real competition wasn't Steve Austin or Colt Cabana, but rather Adam Carolla and Chris Hardwick, two podcast masters who were "must dos" when celebs had something to promote.

In order to get into that rarified podcasting air, I realized early on that the best interviews were always done in person, so I made it a rule to do phone interviews only if there were no other options (guys like Ace Frehley and Jesse Ventura always get call-in passes). As a result, I started carrying my recording gear with me everywhere I went, in a white pillow case (it's durable and flexible), so I was prepared to do interviews no matter where I was.

If I was on a WWE tour and we passed through Detroit, I would go chat with Insane Clown Posse. If I did a festival like Carolina Rebellion with Fozzy, I would arrange a chat with Corey Taylor, Vinnie Paul, or whoever else I knew that was on the bill. Also, by working steadily with the WWE and being in the locker room weekly, I had Kevin Owens on the week after he became the Universal Champion and Seth Rollins the day he came back from a six-month injury. Even though it was a lot more travel and work for me, I was delivering the best guests in the best settings, which translated to excellent show quality and ratings.

Then to take things further, if I could book a cluster of guests to make it worthwhile enough, I traveled to certain cities on my days off. For example, I flew to Chicago to talk to Charlie Benante about the Beatles, Billy Corgan about TNA wrestling, and Bobby Hull about the WHA Winnipeg Jets all in one day. Then I flew to Las Vegas to talk to Nicko McBrain from Iron Maiden, Annie Lobert from Hookers for Jesus, and Disco Inferno from the soup kitchen, then zipped over to New York to chat with Paul Heyman, Jim Breuer, and the Impractical Jokers.

I was going out of my way to get the most interesting and diverse guests, and I didn't care if I had to spend some money in the process. Besides, the cash I spent on airfare or hotel expenses added up to only a small percentage of the increasing ad revenues I was bringing in.

It wasn't easy running the entire *TIJ* organization basically by myself (with some help from my amazing producer, Stacie Parra), and it was a lot of extra work to book the guests or record episodes on the same day as other gigs (tracking a live *Talk Is Jericho* in Toronto with Kevin Owens just a few hours before my main event at Survivor Series 2016 comes to mind). Worse yet was the mental mindfuck when guests cancelled or barely made it in time to do a proper show, like when Meat Loaf got lost for three hours and arrived at the studio only fifty minutes before I had to leave for a flight, or when Kevin Smith was out walking his dog and totally forgot we had arranged to meet that day, or when Ralph Macchio claimed he wanted to do it but bailed every time I gave him a possible date, until I started feeling like a mark and quit asking. But for the most part the stress and extra labor were worth it, because I had now developed a legitimate third source of income and created a whole new cottage industry for myself.

I expanded that industry even further when Norm and I came to an agreement to start The Jericho Network, an offshoot of PodcastOne that was to be operated by me. I would pick the shows and the hosts, make the deals, and decide the content for my network, which had the huge benefit of being under the massive PodcastOne banner, meaning it would attract more advertisers and give the shows a certain prestige right off the bat.

The first podcast on TJN was "Keepin' It 100 with Konnan" and it was a success out of the gate. Others followed, and while some were hits and others were not, all of them were quality programs, with subjects and hosts as diverse as *Talk Is Jericho*. I'm very proud of all the shows on my network, as well as the fact that I have a vehicle to put them on in the first place.

I'm also proud that I've never become complacent. I may be accomplished in wrestling and music, but it doesn't stop me from doing the work required to be an A-list podcaster as well.

You shouldn't be afraid to do the same. Take a chance and expand your horizons, because with hard work you will always succeed.

Okay, now that you've finished this chapter, get back to work! You can read the rest of the book later.

CHAPTER 5

THE RICHARD HAYDEN PRINCIPLE

DON'T TAKE NO FOR AN ANSWER

Well, I won't back down, no I won't back down,
you can stand me up at the gates of hell,
but I won't back down . . .
—TOM PETTY, "I WON'T BACK DOWN"

Who doesn't love the movie *Tommy Boy*? It's by far Chris Farley's best work, boasting a great cast of supporting characters led by the sardonic straight man Richard Hayden, played by David Spade. Hayden has the unenviable job of taking Tommy on a road trip to try and teach him how to be a brake-pad salesman after his father's death. Slowly but surely (don't call me Shirley), Tommy begins to understand the concept of selling the products and selling himself. But he doesn't pick it up all at once, which leads to one of my favorite exchanges in the film when Richard is trying psych him up for the big sales pitch.

"All right, now it's sale time so remember, we don't take no . . ."

"No shit from anyone," Tommy finishes his sentence triumphantly.

"No."

"Umm, we don't take no prisoners?" he retorts hesitantly.

"We don't take no for an answer," sighs an exasperated Richard.

Now think about that phrase, "We don't take no for answer."

Pretty simple in theory, right? Maybe so, but don't get cocky, kid. In reality, it's not as easy as it seems (and I ain't talkin' about *Unmasked*). I warned you earlier in the introduction of this book about the power of the word "no." Usually when we hear that lexeme, something negative happens. It's like just hearing that word gives us permission not to try. And if you don't try, Constant Reader, well, that's the death of your dreams. What you have to realize is that when it comes to your personal and professional goals, there's always a way to get what you want. It just takes some time, creativity, and persistence.

There are tons of examples during my career of me not taking no for an answer, and you can read about them in my other three über-successful books (aka *The Greatest Trilogy in Literary History* or *J. R. R. Tolkien Was a Stupid Idiot Hack*). But rather than retell those tales, I want to do something a little different in this chapter. They say that 90 percent of being a good parent is just showing up. Well, in the worlds of rock 'n' roll and wrestling, 90 percent of the job (at least in terms of the hours you spend) is traveling from one gig to another and getting there in one piece and on time. It was Cooper—Alice—who once said, "They don't pay me for the show, they pay me for the other twenty-two hours before the gig."

Alice has a great point, but I have a couple of other interesting thoughts to share with you that illustrate how you can have a better journey to the gig, just by utilizing a little creativity.

The first classy anecdote deals with a classy problem I once had back in the '90s.

In 1995 I was traveling to Japan every month for WAR (an acronym for the amazingly named Wrestling and Romance), racking up thousands of frequent flyer miles and getting systemwide first-class upgrades in the mail as a result. The upgrades claimed to be good for any international flight, yet whenever I tried to use them, I was told they were ineligible because Wrestling and Romance were buying me the cheapest ticket fares possible. It was frustrating to have this first-class check with nowhere to cash it, so just for fun I would call the airline daily for a week or so before the flight and try to upgrade. Then when they told me my ticket wasn't the right fare class to redeem the certificate, I hung up the phone, and called back instantly. After all, it was a three-hour flight from Calgary to LAX and a twelve-hour flight from LAX to Tokyo (even though there were direct flights leaving from Calgary, WAR still flew me on connecting flights through Los Angeles, but that's another story), so I had nothing to lose, right?

Finally, my persistence paid off one day when I was making my daily play-dumb call and the lady at the end of the line took my upgrade number, messed around on the computer for a minute, and asked what seat I'd like in first class. I couldn't believe I'd actually succeeded for once, and ran around my sparsely furnished apartment doing the "First-Class Dance" (if you wanna see this little jig, Constant Reader, ask me to show it to you the next time I see you) and basking in the glow of my good fortune. I continued calling before every tour, and even though I only got upgraded a few more times, it was a lot better than sitting in middle-seat smoking every flight. More importantly, that experience taught me that certain airline employees can pretty much do whatever they want, and if you keep trying, sooner or later you'll find somebody who can help you get what you need.

Another example of this Airline Enigma happened after I went to the 2016 Rock & Roll Hall of Fame ceremony in New York City with my Wise Cousin Chad. After drinking all night with Lars Ul-rich and Roger Glover of Deep Purple (does your foot hurt from those names I just dropped?), we slept through the alarm and missed our early-morning flights home. My heart started beat-ing faster than Lars's drums on "Dyers Eve" when I remembered that my son Ash had a big football game later that afternoon and I couldn't miss it. Luckily, I was able to quickly rebook another flight that left only an hour after the one I had slept through. But after lazing around the room for a half hour, I realized that I didn't have as much time to make it to the airport as I thought, and scrambled out of the hotel quickly. My flight was leaving out of JFK airport, which was a ways away from our Times Square lodging, as well as the WORST in the United States to check into if you're in a rush.

Besides being one of the only airports in America where you have to check in exactly sixty minutes before your flight (being just one minute late will cause your reservation to automat-ically be cancelled and rebooked), getting from the rental car center to check-in takes at least thirty minutes on the slowest train ever. So even though I got to JFK (and I ain't talkin' about Kevin Costner) about seventy-five minutes before my flight took off, which would be plenty of time in almost any other airport in America, I knew I could still be in trouble.

After getting off the train (that stopped an agonizing half dozen times), I had a sparse fifty minutes to check in and make my flight, knowing that I still had a seven-minute walkrun (that's a new word I just coined) down a winding, outdoor tarp-covered sidewalk. Then there was another escalator and another walkrun (see, that word is a thing now) through the ter-minal, and when I finally arrived at the check-in desk, I had less than forty-five minutes before the plane took off.

I breathlessly explained to the blank-faced lady behind the counter that I was seriously late and needed some help to make the flight, but she told me there was no way I would make it, and that the next plane didn't leave for five hours.

I had two options at this point:

1. Accept Bertha Blankface's answer, concede defeat, and go sit in the concourse for five hours.

OR

2. Take the advice of one Richard Hayden ("We don't take no for an answer") and come up with another option.

I decided to take option two, so I mustered up my courage and asked to speak . . . to a Red Coat.

For those who don't travel a lot, a Red Coat is the supervisor of the check-in folk and is like a mythical creature: rarely seen but with the magical powers to get almost anything done on almost any flight. If you find the right one, they can save your keister, and I needed some serious keister saving right now if I was going to make it back to Tampa in time to see Ash's big game.

A few minutes later (I had about thirty-six minutes before my bird took wing), a pleasant-looking aged Red Coat magically appeared on a cloud before me to assess my situation. She looked into her crystal ball/computer and told me she would try to cast a spell to override the system and see if I could make the flight— but then she couldn't find my reservation.

And that's because there wasn't one.

When I had rebooked my ticket earlier that morning, I was in such a panic that I'd accidentally made the new one for three days later.

"Oh boy . . . .I'm sorry, sir, there's nothing I can do," she said with a sympathetic wince underneath her wizard's hat.

My heart sank like the *Black Pearl* when I realized I was actually going to miss Ash's game . . . until as if on cue, two baggage handlers who looked like Bill and Ted approached me and asked the magic question.

"Are you Chris Jericho?"

I answered that I was and they gave each other high fives with a grin. (Humble Author's note: It always embarrasses me when grown men give each other props for completing the simple task of figuring out that I'm me. I mean come on . . . it's not like they captured a Charizard or something.) But on that day, I could've kissed them, because now that this new shit had come to light, the thaumaturgic Red Coat looked me up and down thoroughly.

"You are Chris Jericho, aren't you?" she said knowingly.

Then she glanced at her watch, which showed thirty-four minutes before the wheels went up, and went back to the crystal ball/computer. She found a seat on the flight I was trying to catch, and two minutes later handed me my boarding pass, as her lowly minion Bertha Blankface looked on in disapproval.

"There's one problem though," Red Coat said. "There's not enough time to check your bag, so you'll have to take it through security yourself and gate check it on the plane."

I almost asked her to repeat herself, as after twenty-six years of traveling through the airports of the world, this was the first time I'd ever been told I could take a checked bag THROUGH TSA. And it was a big-ass bag too, one that weighed about seventy pounds and was a chore for me to lug around. I had no idea how it was going to fit through the X-ray machine, but at that point it was not for me to reason why, it was for me to do or die. So I walkran (I'm adding tenses to this new word that's sweeping the nation) towards the security line, which of course was super long. On top of that, to the surprise of no one, the attendant told me I couldn't take that big of a bag through security. I didn't take no for an answer and told him that the Red Coat necromancer had given me the go-ahead. Thankfully, she materialized behind me and waved her wand, causing the attendant to drop to his knees in fear. Then she led me to the front of the line and bade me farewell. A single tear fell out of my eye as she disappeared in a cloud of smoke, as I knew I would never see this remarkable Red Coat again. But I had to forge on, and with only twenty-five minutes before the eagle unlanded, I hefted my cumbersome suitcase onto the conveyer belt of the security machine.

I was wondering how in the hell this cyclopean bag was gonna fit through the small opening of the X-ray machine, and imagined Andre the Giant's mom during birth as I tried to shove it into the opening. But after a few minor adjustments, I was surprised to find that those X-ray machine tunnels are bigger than I'd thought. I was able to push the case through quite easily, and after dealing with the minor setback of having to remove an economy-sized bottle of Listerine (it is not like it was nitroglycerin . . . or was it?) out of my satchel, I was on my way to the promised land of Flight 1209. My gate was A32 and since I was at A10, I had mere minutes to walkrun (okay, even I'm getting sick of this word) to the gate, dragging the monolithic valise behind me. But after performing the mad dash at a medium pace (and I ain't talkin' about Adam Sandler), I arrived at the gate just as the last passenger was boarding. I flashed my boarding pass to the gate dude who was rocking a baldfro that would've made Larry David proud, but he stopped me and said that my portmanteau wouldn't be permitted on the plane and I'd have to check it.

"That's pretty, pretty, pretty obvious . . ." I muttered as I left the bag at the desk and walked on the plane like Sasha Banks. When I sat down in my seat, the flight attendant inquired if I'd like something to drink and I asked for a coffee.

"I'm sorry, sir, there's none brewed."

I decided to take a chance. After the hassle I'd just endured to make that flight, there was no way I was taking no for an answer when it came to that java! I batted my eyelashes, smiled, and politely asked if there was any way she could please make a quick pot if it wasn't too much trouble. She paused for a second, then said, "Let me see what I can do," and a few minutes later I was taking a sip of Mrs. Folger's finest.

"We don't take no for an answer" flashed through my mind and somewhere in Sandusky, Richard Hayden was fixing his toupee and smiling.

CHAPTER 6

THE NEGRO CASAS PRINCIPLE (AKA THE BAD COW INCIDENT)

KNOW YOUR AUDIENCE

So tell me what you want,
what you really really want . . .
—SPICE GIRLS, "WANNABE"

Water was dripping off the ceiling of the sweaty little arena in Acapulco, streaming down my back in rivulets and making me feel like I was wrestling in the rain.

The ring canvas was as damp as the clothes of the two thousand fans jammed into the mid-sized building getting their weekly *lucha libre* fix. The place was so humid that my hair was plastered to my head like Waldo, and it was all I could do to gulp in enough air to stay conscious. Even though I wrestled in these swampy conditions dozens of times a month, I never quite got used to the swelter. Especially on a night like this when the crowd wasn't nearly as hot as the temperature in the hall.

That's how it goes . . . some nights you get crowds that don't have the energy you want, and the match suffers. Maybe it was the incandescent climate or the fact that there were *lucha* shows every Wednesday and they had seen all of our tricks, but whatever the reason, this crowd wasn't making noise no matter what we did.

Thankfully, one of my opponents in the tag team main event happened to be Negro Casas, the best wrestler you've probably never heard of. He was so good in everything that he did—a true Jedi master of ring psychology—and I could tell that the lack of reaction was frustrating him. We had been doing a match based around quick and intricate *combinacions* (also known as high spots) and the crowd was just dead. They had seen a whole night full of spectacular moves and had reacted favorably, but it was becoming apparent that this wasn't what they wanted from the main event. Negro felt it and since he knew his audience so well, he decided to call an audible.

The planned finish for the second fall of our match was for me to give him a moonsault off the top rope, but when the time came for the fall, he grabbed me in a headlock and whispered in his weird English, "No moonsault. Push me corner and when I hit my partner, roll up me."

As the veteran, it was his job to call the match, so I did what I was told. I worked my way back up onto my feet and pushed Negro off the ropes opposite his corner. When he ran towards me, I sidestepped him and gave him a shove straight into his partner, Gran Markus. The collision drove Markus off the apron to the floor, and Casas stumbled backwards right into my awaiting schoolboy. He whispered to the ref to count to *tres* and the crowd came alive when I got the pin, cheering wildly at how the stupid heels had run into each other like *los Tres Chiflados*.

After the finish, Negro yelled at Markus to come back in the ring and initiated a shoving match with his beefier partner, which made the crowd cheer even more. Then he did something so subtle and genius that I remember every little thing as if it happened only yesterday. With the water still running down the sides of the walls, and the humidity so thick you could cut it with Valyrian steel, Negro yelled at the ring announcer to hand him the microphone.

He grabbed the stick with authority . . . and promptly electrocuted himself.

Now, he didn't actually get shocked like Ace Frehley in Lakeland, circa 1976, but he sold it as if he had. He threw his sweaty hands up in surprise, dropping the mic as quickly as he could. Then he did a little dance with his hands between his knees, like a five-year-old kid who has to go wee-wee, shaking vigorously and making wacky, whimpering noises.

After a night of *quebradoras*, *pescados*, and *tope con hilos*, the biggest reaction of the show was drawn by a guy doing the hippy-hippy shake after pretending to be electrocuted. Once our match started, Negro noticed that the crowd wasn't there to see Cirque du Soleil acrobatics; they were there to see the top-guys entertain them. He was savvy enough to know his audience and change the direction of the match before it was too late. His instincts were right, and they were rewarded by the fans throwing money into the ring afterwards, which in Mexico was the ultimate sign that they felt they had just seen something special. At the time, I didn't fully understand why Negro had made that call, so afterwards in the dressing room I asked him why he had decided to change the course of the match in such a drastic way.

"Okay, explain me," he said with his arms crossed and a vintage Negro whimsical expression on his face. "Sometimes fans don't want technique and high spots. They no understand. But everybody understands how to laugh and enjoy the show. Tonight I give people what they want and make them smile."

He was right and just as in wrestling, in business, and in life as well, you have to know your audience, just like Negro did. What do they want from you? What do they want to hear? Your ability to read the room and adjust accordingly can be the difference between playing on the practice squad or winning the Heisman.

People always ask me if I prefer to be a babyface or a heel. I tell them that it's easier to make people hate you than it is to make them like you, but it's even harder to make them STAY hating you once you get over. But as long as the audience is making noise, I don't really care. Because if they're enjoying themselves, I'm connecting with them, which means they'll continue to pay to see me. And that's the essence of my job.

That's why, no matter what I do outside of WWE, I never downplay my wrestling accomplishments. I'd be crazy not to give the Friends of Jericho some wrestling love in whatever I'm doing, because a certain part of my fan base knows me exclusively from that world. When I'm putting together my lineup for *Talk Is Jericho*, I always make sure to include a healthy dollop of wrestling guests, even though I love the fact that the success of *TIJ* lies in its diversity. I understand that if I expect my wrestling fan base to check out the Kenny G or Heaven's Metal Meltdown episodes, I need to "reward" them with Finn Balor or Roman Reigns shows afterwards. That's because I know my audience.

So does the great Paul McCartney, who when asked about playing new songs in concert, said that whenever he plays a song off his new album, he makes sure to give the audience a "spoonful of sugar" afterwards by performing one of his classics. This allows Paul to promote his new material, but makes sure to give the old-school fans what they want as well. Know your audience and keep them happy.

This principle doesn't only apply to performing in front of an audience. It also applies to one-on-one conversations. What does your boss expect from you? What do you say to your wife after she's spent the last ten minutes telling you about her shitty day? How do you keep people dancing at the party if you're in charge of spinning the platters that matter?

In the WWE, this is especially the case, as it's a well-known fact that you're performing for an audience of one, and the only opinion that matters belongs to Vince McMahon.

After working for him for over seventeen years, I've gotten to know something about this audience of one. They say timing is everything, and with Vince I'll go even further: timing is the only thing. If he looks annoyed, don't approach him no matter how great your idea is. When you do talk to him and he sits in silence after your pitch, you need to fight the urge to fill in the silence, and just let him think.

But the biggest rule when pitching an idea to Mr. McMahon is never, and I mean NEVER, go to him when he's hungry or eating. The guy works harder than anybody I've ever met, so he doesn't get a lot of time for snacking. Not to mention that even at seventy-one years old, he's still built like a shit brickhouse and his diet is probably planned out down to the minute. If he misses that minute, he gets hangry quickly, and who can blame him? I'm smart enough to avoid him when he's in those moods. I don't even want to be in the same room while he's eating, never mind trying to convince him that my latest idea is a genius gift from the wrestling gods. That's the best way to make sure your carefully thought-out storyline doesn't flame out and suffer the same fate as the flight of Icarus.

That's why I waited until the right time to pitch my killer idea for an angle that was to culminate at SummerSlam 2014. I was working a program with Bray Wyatt that had tons of storyline potential, but for some odd reason didn't have much of a story at all. It had begun with a bang tango, when I surprised The Miz on *Raw* with one of my secret returns, which in turn led to The Wyatt Family surprising ME and kicking my ass. But at that point, the storyline part of the story pretty much ended. Despite our constant pitches for the angle to get some direction, it seemed that Vince wanted to keep things basic. . . which I didn't like.

I'm always more effective when I have a detailed angle to work with (see my previous storylines with Shawn Michaels and Rey Mysterio or my latest runs with Dean Ambrose or Kevin Owens for proof) and while my matches with Bray were good, the reasons behind them were almost nonexistent. I wanted to change that and figured out a plan leading to SummerSlam that I was CONVINCED the boss was going to dig.

I knew my audience and I made sure to carefully consider the timing, as I was certain that the key to getting what I wanted was to catch Vince at the right moment. So when I showed up at the arena in Corpus Christi, Texas, for a *Smackdown* taping, I surveyed the landscape and started snooping.

I arrived at 1 p.m. knowing that Vince would still be in the production meeting, going over the show with the writers, agents, and producers. After that initial meeting, there would be a secondary meeting and after that Vince would eat a meal. Then he would be free to talk to the boys . . . or at least the boys he wanted to talk to. Even though Vince had a theoretical open-door policy, in reality it wasn't that easy to get an audience with the audience of one.

Vince is a very intimidating guy, and standing outside his door waiting to talk to him is like waiting to go into the principal's office in junior high school. When you got to the front of the line, it took nerves of steel to muster up the courage to knock and go inside. If Vince wanted to talk, he would give you a big smile and tell you to come in. If he offered up an embrace, that was even better, because he is not a Bayley-type hugger. As a matter of fact, he's quite the opposite—hugs are prime real estate for Vince and he won't fake it. I've seen him strong-arm guys who were going in for the squeeze and it's quite awkward . . . I say this with experience because it's happened to me. My style is to shake somebody's hand first and then pull them in for the clinch and there've been times with Vince where he locked his elbow and slightly pushed my hand back when I was getting a bit too close. So it was a roll of the dice, and you just never knew what you were going to get when you walked in his door.

That day I hedged my bets as much as I could. I'd waited until the second meeting was done and had my idea ready to go with a concise and detailed description. Vince didn't like a bunch of "umms" or "maybes" when you were making your case. The more confident *you* were, the more confident *he* would be in your idea and its potential for success. This is a lesson that applies to life in general as well; confidence is contagious.

But I was prepared and had all the angles covered when I approached his door. However, being the seasoned veteran that I am, I had one more fail-safe in my bag of tricks ready to go before I took the journey to the other side. I was friendly with the entire WWE security staff, including Jimmy Kelly, whose job it was to politely keep anybody out of Vince's office who he didn't want to see. Thankfully, after fifteen years of working in the company, I was one of the chosen ones who had carte blanche to enter Vince's inner sanctum whenever I needed to.

"Has he eaten?" I asked. Jimmy replied that he had and more importantly, was in a good mood.

With that knowledge, it was time to take a chance (and I ain't talking about Savatage) and jump in headfirst.

I rapped on the door, walked inside (I always felt like I was barging in or interrupting whenever I went into his office) and surveyed the situation. I had entered a large conference room with lines of tables leading all the way to the back of the room, and sitting at the last table farthest away from the door was Vince . . . and his heir apparent, Triple H.

The fact that HHH was there was a red flag. I always worked better with Vince when it was just the two of us in the room. If I had known he wasn't alone, I would've waited.

However, I had already jumped off the diving board and there was no turning back now.

"Oh come on . . . " Vince said in mock disgust when he saw me, a private joke between us every time I came in to talk with him.

He got a kick out of acting like I was the last person in the world he wanted to see, even though he had told me many times, "Anytime you have anything you want to talk about . . . ANY-THING . . . come find me."

As a result, I was usually in his office on a weekly basis for one reason or another. However, having Triple H in the room now threw me off my game (pun intended) slightly and I felt a little self-conscious walking past the rows of tables towards the front.

Vince stood up with a big smile and shook my hand . . . but didn't bring me in for a hug. That was another bad sign.

"Hey, boss, I've got this really cool idea for Wyatt and me for SummerSlam that I want to run past you."

"Sounds great, junior." (He loves calling me that, after I used it as an insult in the early 2000s. I think he gets a kick out of it because he's a junior himself and apparently hates being referred to as such.) "Do you mind if Paul stays?"

Talk about a loaded question. I really didn't want Paul (Triple H) to stick around, as his presence threw a monkey wrench into my pitch. But what choice did I have? If I said no, it would be uncomfortable and an insult towards HHH and possibly an insult to Vince too. Besides, it was my fault for not asking Jimmy Kelly if Vince was alone in the room before I went in. But it was too late for that now and besides, I was Chris Jericho! I had helped write some of the best storylines in WWE history and I knew I could sell Vince on this one, no matter if HHH, Outback Jack, or Pauly Shore were in that damn room.

"Of course he can stay. I'd like his input too," I lied.

Once again, I knew my audience and figured that Vince wanted Paul in the room in the first place or he wouldn't have asked. So by agreeing to have him there, I was showing some confidence and being a team player. Or something like that.

With the first hurdle cleared, I jumped right into my pitch.

"Okay, so every week Y2J has been getting attacked by Bray Wyatt and The Wyatt Family," I said. "I clearly need some help, but I've been such an asshole over the last few years that nobody trusts me enough to have my back. So I thought it would be great if—"

"Hold on a second, Chris," Vince interrupted. "Paul, can you grab that other steak for me please? I'm still hungry."

Fuck.

In my head those three words reverberated across the room with an echo effect like a cheesy radio ad for a *Monster Jam* show.

"I'm still hungry . . . Hungry . . . HUNGRY!"

Right then I knew I was in trouble. Vince would now be concentrating more on his meal than my pitch. Having the distraction of HHH in the room was nothing compared to the distraction of Vince's appetite.

Paul grabbed a plate from another table and took it over to the boss. It was steak and broccoli, covered in Saran Wrap with VINCE—2 PM written on it in black Sharpie. It seemed that the steak had been cooked at 2 p.m., and since it was almost 3 p.m. it was time to eat it before it got (stone) cold. And that's what Vince was about to do.

"Continue," he said, beckoning as he unwrapped his meaty treasure, grabbed a fork, and dug in.

I continued with my spiel, but I felt like Indiana Jones trying to outrun the boulder in the temple. I'd have to pick up the pace or risk being run over by the giant rock that was Vince's appetite.

So I continued, throwing caution to the wind. Surely if I could best locker room politics and Bill Goldberg in a backstage kerfuffle, I could best Vince McMahon's ravenousness as well!

"Okay, as I was saying, nobody in the WWE locker room trusts me enough to have my back, because I've turned on everybody I've ever teamed with in the past. So next week on *Raw*, I get attacked and run over by the Wyatts again. They leave me lying and I have to get helped out of the ring. A few segments later, I'm getting tended to in the trainer's room and I ask the doctors to leave so I can make a phone call. I want to get in contact with the only guy I know who is crazier than me. The only guy who has turned on more partners and has had as many ups and down in the WWE as me. A guy who I can't stand and whose life I made a living hell. A man I hate with every bone in my body, but who I have the ultimate respect for. A man who I know would go to hell and back with me if I could convince him my intentions were true.

"I would pick up the phone and say, 'Operator . . . give me the number for the HBK Ranch in Abilene, Texas.'"

With that bombshell, I let the words hang in the air, expecting a big reaction from the old man. All I got was the sound of Vince chewing on his steak, and he only looked up briefly in acknowledgment.

But I was deep into the groove and continued to excitedly unravel the rest of my tale.

"So the next week I'm in the middle of the ring. I say I made the call and left a message extending the invite for HBK to come to the arena so I could explain myself, and even left a first-class plane ticket under his name at the airport. I don't know if he's here or not, but I'm praying that he is, because there's nobody else I can turn to. I know if I could just talk to him face to face, he would see the sincerity in my eyes and hear it in my voice that I really need his help."

After a dramatic pause, the iconic "Sexy Boy" music would play and The Heartbreak Kid, Shawn Michaels, my biggest WWE rival and the greatest of all time, would come out onto the stage. He would prance down to the ring as only he could, but remain silent as I explained that even though we had tortured each other for years, he was the only man I wanted on my side as I fought the epitome of evil. I was envisioning something out of an old Western, where the sheriff would recruit the lethal gunslinger he had put in jail twenty years earlier to help him stop the band of outlaws that were threatening the safety of his town.

Shawn would stand in silence contemplating my request, and then slowly lift the microphone to his mouth to respond. But before he could say a word, the lights would go out and The Wyatt Family's "horror graphic" would play. The lights would come back on revealing all three of them standing in the ring surrounding us. I envisioned the crowd going nuts at that point, as the bad guys moved in to attack.

They would beat me down as Shawn looked on in silence, and then turn their attention to him. HBK would turn his back to leave, with the crowd begging him to get involved. When the reaction was at its highest, Shawn would suddenly spin around and dole out some Sweet Chin Music to Erick Rowan. Then Bray and Harper would attack, but Shawn would duck out of the way, nail Harper with a superkick, and force Wyatt to powder out of the ring. At this point, Shawn would grab the mic and say, "Jericho, after being attacked by those slugs, if you want me to watch your back . . . YOU GOT IT!"

I loved the fact that we would never know what Shawn was going to say before the Wyatts got involved. He might've agreed to help me or told me to go to hell, but after the Wyatts attacked him what he thought of me was irrelevant; now he had a fight of his own to deal with.

The next week we would have another ring confrontation, which would lead to us clearing the ring and then backing into each other. Of course, we would turn around quickly and Shawn would tease the superkick as I threw up my hands in defense. The tension would build until we eventually shook hands in the ring, showing the world that we were on the same team. Birds would sing, babies would laugh, and the sun would forever shine with the revelation that the first-ever alliance between Michaels and Jericho was going to happen! This would all lead to Bray Wyatt with his Family in his corner versus Chris Jericho with HBK in his corner at SummerSlam.

Phew! Sounds pretty damn good, right? Thank you, Constant Reader. I felt the same way . . . but did Vince agree?

"Well," I said as straight fire burned in the corners of the room from the heat of my marvelous brainchild, "what do you think?"

I couldn't wait to hear him say how much he loved my amazing idea and find out what thoughts he had to make it better.

Except he didn't say anything.

Nothing. Nada. Zilch. Bupkus. Zip. Goose Egg. Diddly. Nought. Bagatelle.

He just slowly chewed his food, staring off at an unidentified object in the corner of the room as if he were playing Pokéman Go. When he swallowed, an epiphany seemed to hit him as he looked up from his steak and made a strange face.

I thought to myself, *His next words are gonna blow me away*, and they did, but not in the way I expected.

"Bad Cow."

Exsqueeze me? Baking powder?

"Sorry, Vince?"

"Bad COW," he repeated, with greater emphasis.

Yeah, I caught that the first time. But I still had no idea what the fuck he was talking about.

"BAD COW," he said emphatically for a third time before elaborating. "This steak is too tough and bland. It's from a Bad Cow."

Now out of all the responses that I might've expected to hear about my killer idea . . . let's just say that a thousand monkeys could've typed for a thousand years and they wouldn't have come up with that piece of horseshit.

"I'm sorry that you've eaten some ummm . . . Bad Cow, Vince, but what did you think about my idea?"

He stared at me, then back at the cursed chunk of half-eaten meat that had ruined my presentation and muttered, "What else ya got?"

If the "Bad Cow" comment wasn't enough to hammer home the fact that my idea was dead in the water, the "What else ya got?" gibe was the final kick to my creative plums.

"Well?" he said looking at me expectantly.

"Yeah, I really don't have anything else, Vince. That was pretty much all I had, and I put a lot of time into putting it together."

"Well damn it, Chris, you need to have multiple ideas when you come see me. Besides, I don't think Shawn would be interested in this anyway."

I had one last hope. HHH and HBK were the oldest and best of friends. Maybe Paul would jump at the chance to bring his buddy back for another money-making run.

"Yeah, I don't think he's even available," H chimed in, bursting my bubbleski. I'd have happily punched him in his huge honker at that moment, considering the mood I was in. (Angry Author's note: Not only was Shawn available, but he was booked to be in Los Angeles the morning of SummerSlam to do a Q&A at the WWE Axxess fan festival.)

Of course it wasn't HHH's fault that Vince didn't go for it and it wasn't that Bad Cow's fault. I even felt bad for the poor thing. After all, it had been groomed its whole life for the sole purpose of being a tasty meal for someone. And now, not only had it failed miserably in its life's mission, but thanks to this book, it's being insulted and vilified long after its bloody death in the abattoir.

I'm sorry, Madam Bad Cow.

It was really my fault for not choosing a better time to approach Vince to get his undivided attention. I didn't take heed of my own words and previous experiences to create the best environment for success, and as a result I failed to get what I wanted. Listen to these words, Constant Reader, and please don't let the same fate befall you. Don't get BadCowed like I did.

Can we at least get that phrase trending on Twitter?

#BadCowed

CHAPTER 7

THE YODA PRINCIPLE

THERE IS NO TRY . . . ONLY DO

Day after day I get up and I say,
I better do it again . . .
—THE KINKS, "DO IT AGAIN"

Growing up in the early '80s, I was into a lot of things: the Beatles, comic books, GI Joe action figures, *Cracked Magazine,* and hockey cards, but there was one pop cultural, uh, force, that had more impact on me and my friends than anything else. A movie that shaped and molded us with the messages contained dealing with the power of good and evil and the ability of one person to make a difference. Plus, it had cool-looking aliens and Han fuckin' Solo! Constant Reader, of course I'm talking about *Star Wars* and its sequels, *The Empire Strikes Back* and *Return of the Jedi.*

Out of all the wisdom in those movies, the most powerful lessons came from the diminutive Jedi master, Yoda. Despite his small stature, greenish hue, and a Broken Matt Hardy–style butchery of the English language, Yoda spouted off more inspirational one-liners than Confucius himself. While there are quite a few gems to choose from, the one that stayed with me the most was the simple yet effective statement of, "There is no try, only do."

(Surprised Editor's note: After doing some research, I found out that the actual quote is "Do or do not. There is no try." I had no idea I was misquoting Yoda all these years, but I've decided to keep it the way I remembered it because it's my book. If you don't like it, go read an Eckhart Tolle essay.)

A better motto for our lives I cannot think, as it encapsulates the theme of this entire book. It's a subtle yet important rule, but it requires a little bit of mental jujitsu. Let's say there's a goal you haven't accomplished. Tell yourself you're GOING to do it, and know it's just a matter of time until you figure out when and how. That works a lot better than saying to yourself you'll "try," which introduces the possibility of failure right from jump street.

To put it another way, if you think you can do something, adopt the Nike motto of "Just do it" and damn the torpedoes (and I ain't talkin' about Tom Petty) until it's done. Saying you'll try puts you in a weak place mentally and acknowledges you might not be ready to tackle the task at hand. You're better off carefully considering the logistics of how to do something and then doing it, and leave trying out of the equation altogether.

I consider myself a perfectionist. I want everything I do to be the best it can be, and if it's not, I won't be happy. At the same time, in order for me to do my best in the first place, I need to start somewhere, and that begins with putting myself out there at all times.

Consider a friend of mine from Winnipeg that I've known since we were literally babies, who was already one of the best guitar players in town at the tender age of fifteen. He was a natural virtuoso who could play any song in any style, but refused to play live gigs because he perpetually felt he wasn't ready. I personally think he didn't want to play out because he was afraid of negative feedback, and to this day, he still hasn't been in a steady full-time band because of those inhibitions. Even with all that natural talent, he won't succeed because he doesn't try . . . and therefore will never DO.

But to me, the Yoda way is the best way to live; skip the "trying" and go straight to the "doing." Yes, there will be mistakes, but those errors will eventually teach you to be your best. To do something half-assed, or even worse, being too afraid to do something in the first place, are the ultimate sins in my world. I'd rather do something and fail (look in the *Shitty TV Show Dictionary* under "Celebrity Duets" for an example) than sit on the sidelines because I was too afraid.

When I finally decided to do *Dancing with the Stars* after turning down two previous invites, I remember thinking, *Okay, I'm gonna give this a DO* (see what I did there?), because I had no interest in just attempting it. If I was going be involved with this show, I was going to DO it to the best of my ability. I'd never danced before but I wasn't going to use that as an excuse, because once I agreed to be on the show, my only option was success. In eliminating the concept of "trying," I had trained myself over the years that I could do anything I set my mind to. And while I didn't win *DWTS*, I lasted seven weeks and did a pretty damn solid job. Plus, I found out that I looked damn good in a Mexican matador outfit *and* made friends with Sugar Ray Leonard, so it was a definite win.

When I was auditioning heavily in Los Angeles in 2006, my acting coach, Kirk Baltz, told me that the rule for answering inquiries from producers about any special skills I might have was to respond with a resounding YES.

"Chris, can you sky dive?"

"Yes."

"Can you speak Swahili?"

"*Ndiyo.*"

"Can you tie your shmeckel into a tidy Christmas bow?"

"Yes, as a matter of fact, it's in a double fisherman's now."

Say yes first and learn how second, because you don't want to lose out on an opportunity to play Reg Dunlop in a *Slap Shot* remake because you can't skate, or a part in *Zoolander 2* because you're not funny (that didn't stop the actual movie). Your overall attitude should be "Yes I can!" (and I ain't talkin' about Sammy Davis Jr.), because you really can do anything you want; you just have to get off your tuchas and do it!

In the summer of 2014, when I was working the program with Bray Wyatt, our first few PPV matches went okay, but I knew we had the potential to pull off something better. I really wanted our third encounter to stand out, so when I heard that the blow-off match was going to be in a cage on *Raw*, I decided I wanted to do a crossbody off the top of it.

I hadn't done this since 1993, twenty-one years earlier, but I knew I could still pull it off. Plus, it was a no-brainer that the death-defying maneuver would shock people and tear the house down if we put it in the right place at the right time. I pitched the idea to our match producer, Arn Anderson, and he brought up a really good question about the psychology behind the move. Why would I jump off the top of the cage, when I could just climb down to the floor instead and win the match? It was a valid point, so I told him that in my mind the rest of The Wyatt Family would be at the bottom of the cage slamming chairs against the side and blocking my escape, which would force me to have to soar down onto Bray. Arn liked it, and with his blessing I went to pitch it to Vince.

Vince agreed with the idea, except he didn't want the Wyatts to have chairs and had some hesitations as to whether the dive would be safe.

"Maybe you should put the crash pads down and try it first before the show?" he asked sternly.

"No, boss, I'd rather just get up there and do it," I replied confidently.

Even though it had been over two decades since I'd performed the risky move (and I wasn't twenty-two years old anymore), I had faith that I could do it again without any problems.

Before I got into the business, I used to hang around at a Gold's Gym in Winnipeg and watch the WWE wrestlers working out when they were in town. I was a huge Shawn Michaels fan and was obsessed with the fact he could do a backflip from the top rope, so when I saw him training one afternoon before the show, I interrupted his workout and asked him how he did it.

"You just gotta get up there and do it, brother," he said.

Later that night on *Raw*, I heard Shawn's words echoing inside my head as I climbed to the top of the cage with Wyatt lying on the canvas some fifteen feet below me. When we'd discussed the spot earlier he seemed a little hesitant, and I don't blame him. It wasn't because he didn't want to do it, but I'm sure the thought of catching a 210-pound man hurtling down from the sky at lightning speed was a daunting proposal, to say the least. But as I perched on top of the cage, I could see in his body language that he was ready to catch me . . . and by cracky I was ready to fly!

Cage matches are always fun and easy, because all you have to do is utilize the gimmick and try to get out of the cage. Anytime you head towards the door or begin scaling the chain-link wall, the people "always go banana" (Pat Patterson™), so you build the whole match around that. The crowd that night in Baltimore was no different, and as soon as I started climbing up the structure, they began to rumble. By the time I got to the top and swung my leg over the attached truss with Wyatt still prone on the mat below, the crowd was screaming like Rob Halford on the *Screaming for Vengeance* album. They were convinced that this was the finish, and I was going to win the match by scaling down to the ground below. Then just as planned, the evil Harper and Rowan made their way to my side of the cage and started beating on the structure like madmen.

I took a look down, decided I didn't want any piece of the fugly behemoths below, and swung my leg back over the truss. But instead of descending back into the ring, I crouched on the steel beam for a moment and then slowly rose to my full height, with the crowd rising behind me in disbelief. Nobody believed that I was crazy enough to actually jump.

Earlier in the day, I had stood on top of the corner of the cage, holding on to the cable that raised and lowered the framework. I'm not afraid to tell you that I was pretty freaked out standing on that beam in the middle of a completely empty arena. But now the venue was packed with twelve thousand screaming Baltimoreans (is that a word?), and I wasn't freaked out at all. As a matter of fact, I felt pretty BMF standing there with all eyes on me as I stared death in the face. One false move and I could get seriously hurt, or worse. But if this went as planned, it would add another feather into the well-stocked plumage of my Joey Belladonna–style WWE headdress, and that alone made it dangerous but worth the risk (and I ain't talkin' about Ratt).

Years earlier, Vince had taught me to pause before (and after) an important high spot during a match, to give the crowd ample time to slap their friends sitting beside them on the shoulder and say, "Can you believe he's going to do this?" With that advice in mind, I waited for an extra ten seconds as the crowd went wild with expectation. I was feeling a little hesitant, but before I jumped I noticed a tiny figure on each side of my head.

"There is no try, only do," Yoda said to me looking up from my left shoulder.

"You're fucking crazy," Axl Rose bellowed up from my right.

I decided to go with Yoda's advice and flicked Axl off my shoulder. He screamed all the way back down to the jungle, where he exploded into a puff of dust and bones. Sorry, man, I still think about you.

With all my doubts dispelled, I took a deep breath and prepared for take-off. But just before I launched myself, I thought of another pertinent Shawn Michaels moment. When he had his triumphant return match against HHH at SummerSlam 2002, the high point of the contest came when he was about to drop an elbow from the top of a ladder onto a table on the floor. But right before he made the leap of faith, he looked at the crowd, shrugged his shoulders as if to say "What are you gonna do?" and jumped into WWE history. If it was good enough for HBK, it was good enough for me, so I shrugged my shoulders in a "Wha' happen?" homage to the master and dove into the air.

The tagline on the poster for the original 1978 Christopher Reeve *Superman* movie was "You'll believe a man can fly." Well, you didn't have to Netflix and chill to see a man flying in Baltimore that night, 'cause I was super, man!

My descent felt like it took thirty seconds to complete, and I might as well have been skydiving out of a plane. I flew towards Wyatt in seeming half time, as he moved directly under me until he was in perfect position to make the catch. Then I collided directly with his 285-pound form and we went down hard. It was like one of those Instagram videos that starts in slow motion but speeds up at the end . . . and it was awesome.

Even though Bray caught me perfectly and protected me from the potentially hazardous high spot, I still did a quick subconscious body check. After assessing that I had splashed down safely with no injuries, I gave myself a self–high five in honor of the DDP Yoga that had made the leap possible.

When it was all said and done, I had taken a chance to entertain the fans and to prove something to myself and the world. I showed that even though I was in my forties, I could still do anything I damn well pleased in the ring, because I believed in myself and didn't get hung up on wanting to "try" things.

That's because I was too busy doing them.

CHAPTER 8

THE PAUL STANLEY PRINCIPLE

ELIMINATE NEGATIVITY

I'm never gonna run,
I'm never gonna tell myself a lie . . .
—KISS, "MY WAY"

Since you're reading this book, you probably know I'm a massive KISS fan, and Paul Stanley was one of my biggest influences both as a performer and a motivator when I was growing up. Much like me, he totally believed in himself and always went the extra mile to entertain. Throughout my career, I've borrowed little tricks from Paul as an entertainer, but it was his attitude towards life that influenced me the most. To the point that the words I heard him say almost thirty years ago stuck with me and helped shape me into the person I am today.

During the 1988 documentary *The Decline of Western Civilization Part II: The Metal Years,"* Paul is being interviewed while lying in bed surrounded by a gaggle of half-naked gorgeous chicks (as you do). When director (and *Talk Is Jericho* alumna) Penelope Spheeris asks him if he has any advice for kids trying to make it in show biz, he replies, "The only people that are ever gonna tell ya you can't accomplish something are the ones who failed. I'm not here to tell you that you can't do something, 'cause I did it . . . you can do it."

For the record, I didn't have to rewatch the movie or google that quote when I wrote it down right now. I know it by heart and have since I first heard it in '88. Actually, I've used that quote so many times in my own interviews that people think I said it first. Well, I must confess for the record that I didn't coin the phrase, and I guess I owe the Starchild some royalties for that one.

Now, for a thought experiment. I ask you, Constant Reader, to imagine how a seventeen-year-old Chris Irvine with big dreams and no clue how to achieve them must've felt when he first heard this quote. They were powerful words with a powerful message that was tailor-made for a kid like me, who was being laughed at by almost everyone who heard about my life plans. After hearing Paul's wisdom, I had a strong defense against anybody who told me I couldn't accomplish what I wanted. One of the biggest rock stars in history was giving me permission to stick my middle finger into the faces of any Abner Devereaux's who weren't on my side. From that point on, I mentally gave the finger to my detractors like I was Stone Cold Steve Austin in 1998, and I've never stopped since. As a matter of fact, if you're reading this book wondering why Chris Jericho of all people is writing a self-help book, well, I'm giving you a belletristic bird right now!

Hopefully, if you're hearing Paul's words for the first time, you're experiencing the same thing I did back in '88. Maybe you will also experience the sense of empowerment you need to ignore all your doubters and haters. Let's face it, we all only have so much mental energy to spend, so why waste it worrying about the people who doubt you? Who gives a shit what they think?

Forget them, eliminate their negativity, and put that mental energy to better use, like achieving your goals and making your dreams a reality.

Paul's quote meant more to me than every one of Jack Handey's "Deep Thoughts" and was more powerful than three (maybe four) of the Ten Commandments. As a matter of fact, they might as well have been written on tablets and given to me by Moses on the mount . . . if Moses was about to mount a gaggle of scantily clad stable maids that surrounded him on a bed of hay.

Armed with Paul's verbal ammo, I threw myself into everything I did with passion and effort, knowing that the biggest obstacle to reaching a seemingly unattainable goal was a lack of self-confidence. And the biggest roadblocks to that self-confidence are the people who doubt you. Therefore, if you want to succeed, you have to eliminate negative influences in your life before they drag you down.

We had a guy who played in Fozzy for a few years (who shall remain nameless, faceless) say to us after we fired him, "Come on, guys. You honestly don't believe Fozzy is ever going to get any bigger than you are now, do you?"

We most certainly did, and his negativity and lack of belief were two of the reasons we sacked him. We strived to get bigger almost just to spite him, and since then we've toured the world with Metallica, KISS, and Shinedown, played to hundreds of thousands of amazing fans, and our last record, "Do You Wanna Start a War," debuted at number 54 on the Billboard Top 200. I'd say we proved his naysaying ass wrong, haven't we?

"The only people that are ever gonna tell ya you can't accomplish something are the ones who failed." Those words have become a mantra for my life and everything I ever dreamed of doing when I was a kid—like being a father, husband, wrestler, musician, author, actor, podcaster, comedian, butcher, baker, and candlestick maker—I've done (actually, I've never made a damn candle in my life). Besides being the first Canadian James Bond AND an adventuring archaeologist named Indiana

Jonesicho, I've done pretty much everything I ever wanted to do, all with the help of Paul's wise words.

Another dream of mine was to someday actually meet Paul Stanley himself.

I even came up with this reverie that Paul would someday have a son who was into wrestling and would be a fan of mine, which would lead to me finally hanging out with my hero. Funnily enough, that did kind of happen to me backstage at an Iron Maiden show in Milwaukee in 2000, when I was recognized by guitarist Adrian Smith's wife, because their son was a big WWE fan. Ten minutes later, I was talking to the shocked young lad after waking him out of his deep sleep, thousands of miles away in England. I ended up getting invited to watch Maiden play from the side of the stage, and hung out in their dressing room afterwards. I've been buds with Adrian and the entire Maiden organization ever since. (I even got an Eddie-themed Christmas card from them one year.)

Although I was friends with the Smiths, my dream of becoming chummy with the Stanleys never came to fruition. Adrian, Slash, Chad Smith of the Red Hot Chili Peppers, and Phil Campbell from Motörhead all had kids that were into wrestling, but I never heard a thing about Paul's children showing any interest. I slowly gave up on the "his kids like WWE" plan and started to imagine other ways I could strike up a relationship with Paul.

Maybe Fozzy would open for KISS, or I would get a job as a gas-meter checker (shout out to Rybo) in Paul's neighborhood. Perhaps I could become a Jehovah's Witness and deliver a copy of *The Watchtower* to his door?

But none of those ever came to fruition, although I came close to meeting him in 2014 when he was booked on *Talk Is Jericho* during a promotional tour for his autobiography. However, he cancelled just a few hours beforehand and I was crushed. Why would he blow me off so close to showtime? I was really disappointed and resigned myself to the fact that we'd never meet face to face.

Then IT happened, like an RKO #outtanowhere.

I was in the dressing room after a *Raw* taping in August of 2014, when I overheard a couple of the refs talking about how a guy from KISS was asking for a birthday video message for his son from John Cena. That guy was Paul Stanley.

"Hold on, what did you just say?" I asked my old friend and favorite referee, Charles Robinson.

"Apparently, Paul Stanley's son is a big WWE fan and wants a video greeting from Cena as a birthday present."

That was all I needed to hear! If Paul's son was a WWE fan, then that would mean he might know me as well, right?? My crazy dream might come true yet!

Charles told me that Dale Torborg, who had played The KISS Demon in WCW and was tight with the band, had gotten the request from Paul and called to ask for help. I told him I was the guy for the job and would get it done immediately.

I found John changing in a room down the hall and asked him if he could do me a favor and wish a friend of mine happy birthday. Cena was more than gracious and delivered a great thirty-second birthday promo in one take. I grabbed Dale's number and texted him the video, along with a written message of my own thanking Paul for his words of advice all those years ago and congratulating him on his decades of success. Dale agreed to forward both texts to Paul and I figured that was the last of it.

A few days later, I was outside cooking my kids some steak on the grill (I'm a barbequing ninja), when my cell phone rang. It came up as NO CALLER ID so I ignored it. After accidentally tweeting my phone number a few years earlier, I still get the occasional call from random fans, so I never answer unidentified numbers. A few minutes later, I got a text from Torborg saying that Paul loved the video and was planning on calling me to say thanks.

Stop! Hold on! Stay in control.

Did he just say that Paul Stanley was GOING TO CALL ME??

I reread the text and indeed that's what Dale had written. I jumped out of my nonexistent socks, ate my nonexistent hat, and started partying like it was 1999. I couldn't believe what was happening. After all those years and that *Talk Is Jericho* close call at the PodcastOne studios, was I finally going to get my chance to speak to the man himself? Then a scary thought hit me like a ton of bricks (and I ain't talkin' about Metal Church) as a wave of slight nausea cascaded through my stomach.

What if he already called? I thought to myself as a bead of sweat rolled down my forehead. I mean I had only missed the one call and the caller hadn't left a message . . . or had they? I checked my phone to see and noticed a new voice message in the box.

I pressed play on the message arrow and almost collapsed in mortification at what I heard.

"Hey, Chris . . ." a deep, confident New York–accented voice said. After hearing it on albums and in concert for years, I knew instantly who it was.

". . . it's Paul Stanley."

I fell to my knees and screamed, "NOOOOOOO" at the sky like Captain Kirk in *Star Trek II: The Wrath of Khan.*

"I'm just calling to thank you for helping me out—my son is gonna love the video! I want to talk to you . . . and I'm sure you want to talk to me too. I'll bet you're kicking yourself that you missed this call, but I'll try again later."

Kicking myself was an understatement. I was so despondent that if I could've fed myself into a Fargo-style woodchipper, I would've. I instantly called Torborg and asked him to tell Paul to call me back as soon as he could. Then I finished grilling up the steaks and waited . . . and waited . . . and waited. I was sure that Paul would call me back eventually, but as Tom Petty once said, "The waiting is the hardest part." And he wasn't effen' kidding.

I mean, it was worse than waiting for the hot girl you met the night before at Applebee's to call you back after you took a chance and left her a message. It was torturous; I must've checked the clock a half dozen times within the next minute.

Finally, after a few more minutes the phone rang and the NO CALLER ID warning popped up again, so I took a deep breath, and after waiting two more rings for cool points, I answered. It was Paul, and the following twenty-minute conversation we had couldn't have gone better. It took me a few minutes to get the fanboy nervousness out of my system, but once I did we had a great chat about our kids, their birthdays, wrestling, and of course music. I offered to send his son Colin a special present from my private collection, so Paul gave me his cell phone number, email address, physical address and agreed to do *Talk Is Jericho* anytime, which was huge for me. I found him to be a genuinely cool cat, and we got along right off the bat. He must've felt the same way, as five minutes later he emailed me to say that his son was a fan of mine as well and wondered if I could do a birthday greeting for him too.

Damn right I could and couldn't wait to oblige. I laid down a two-minute-long *Raw*-worthy promo on my phone, wishing him a happy birthday and saying that I'd spoken to Vince McMahon about making him an honorary WWE superstar. Then I remarked that if he was going to be an honorary superstar, he needed a superstar outfit and held up my WrestleMania 20 blue-and-silver tights (with matching ring jacket of course), saying they were now his. (Helpful Author's note: This was the outfit I wore against Christian during our WrestleMania 20 match in Madison Square Garden.) After watching it back to make sure it was perfect, I emailed the greeting over to Paul, then packaged up the gear and shipped it to his place.

A few days later, he sent me a video of Colin watching my video. The kid freaked out when I said his name and lost it completely when he took my costume out of the box, just as I held up the tights on my video. Paul reiterated that the costume was worn at WrestleMania in MADISON SQUARE GARDEN, which was sacred ground for both KISS fans and WWE fans alike. Colin put on the gear as fast as he could and despite the fact that the costume hung on him like Rey Mysterio wearing The Big Show's bathrobe, proceeded to throw a picture-perfect air dropkick on his bed. It was an awesome feeling knowing I had made both the kid's and his father's day, and a better feeling knowing that as of that moment, Paul Stanley was more than a hero . . . he was now my friend.

Paul and I have gotten pretty close over the last few years, and he even invited my wife Jessica and me to his ten-year wedding vow renewal, which was a huge honor. It was a great night with many great stories that I'll keep between us, but I will say this: you ain't seen nothing until you've seen Gene Simmons do the twist on a wedding dance floor. He's amazing and his moves are radioactive!

CHAPTER 9

THE VIV SAVAGE PRINCIPLE

HAVE A GOOD TIME ALL THE TIME

We're here for a good time, not a long time,
so have a good time, the sun can't shine every day . . .

—TROOPER, "WE'RE HERE FOR A GOOD TIME"

Spinal Tap's portly keyboard player, Viv Savage, gave one of the best pieces of advice in cinematic history, when documentarian Marty DiBergi asked him what his creed for life was.

"Have a good time, all the time . . . that's my philosophy Marty."

Pretty self-explanatory, right?

You have to love what you do and do what you love and if you don't, then make a change. It doesn't get much easier than that, does it? Whatever your passion might be, no matter how big or how small, no matter how far-fetched or obvious, you owe it to yourself to pursue it with everything you've got.

I remember in the mid-'90s when I was living in Calgary but working in Mexico, I made the cardinal mistake of falling in love while still making my way up the ladder. I was feeling sad about leaving my girl to go back to wrestle in Mexico for another couple of months and asked my best friend (and roommate at the time), "Dr. Luther" Lenny Olson, for his advice. His response was quick and Viv Savage–esque: "Be where you wanna be."

I took those words to heart and decided I wanted be in Mexico, so I broke up with the girl and stuck with my plans to further my career. Lenny and Viv were absolutely right: Life is too short to be unhappy with your surroundings and what you're doing, so no matter what your circumstances are there's always a way to make things better. Never be afraid to go out on a limb to make each day a special one that you'll never forget.

In the summer of 2015, I was on a short WWE tour of Japan made up of two sold-out shows in Sumo Hall in Tokyo. I had a pair of matches, one with Finn Balor, one with Neville, and both tore down the house. It's always an honor for me to return to Japan after basically growing up there in the '90s, and I've done a total of forty-eight tours (and counting) in the country over the years. I put great importance on those matches and feel a huge responsibility to put on the best show I can, both for myself and the fans who have been following me since my first Japanese tour back in 1991.

So after two great shows, I was feeling pretty celebratory and wanted to have a couple drinks on the Tokyo town. Thankfully, a few of the lads wanted to join me, so I put together the motley crew of Xavier Woods, Eddie and Orlando Colon, and WWE doctor Chris Amann. We ended up hooking up with a dude who had a connection at the hottest club in Tokyo, which boasted a private, luxurious karaoke room. Add in some froot fans we met at the bar and multiple bottles of Grey Goose, and suddenly you had the perfect recipe for an awesome night. After a great karaoke session featuring classic renditions of songs by Journey, Player, Whitesnake, the Backstreet Boys, Dokken (for the Doc), Taylor Swift, and an amazing version of Ebony and Ivory with Woods and me singing in perfect harmony (I was Ebony), the club provided a stretch limo for us to get back to the hotel.

When we pulled up at the front doors of the hotel, I was in full Keith Richards mode complete with aviator shades, a cigarette, a scarf, and a bottle of anything in hand. I swaggered out of the limo with a cocky smile and was captured perfectly on film by Orlando. I'm sure it would've been a much easier flight home if I had gone to bed early rather than partying until dawn, but that wouldn't have made as good of a story, now would it?

However, I wasn't always so Keith suave and Richards debonair when I was having a good time all the time. Back in 2014, I was taking a red-eye home from Portland, Oregon, after a *Raw* taping, with Kevin Nash, Hulk Hogan, and John Laurinaitis and I happened to be sitting next to Nash. The flight to Atlanta was five hours long and I had planned to sleep the whole way, but one thing led to another and Big Kev and I started having a few cocktails. I ordered Yeah Boys (Grey Goose and ice, as described in my renowned cocktail book, *Best in the World*) for the both of us, and off we went into the great wide open.

We ended up hanging in the galley of the plane with Hulk (who had gladly signed autographs and taken pictures with almost every passenger on the plane at that point), having a few laughs, and of course a few more cocktails. It was a cool experience, as I'd never really hung out with Hulk and Kevin before. We had been in the trenches together in WCW, but I was pretty much persona non grata back then and we didn't run in the same circles. But as S. E. Hinton once wrote, "that was then, this is now," and at this point we were three former WWE world champions flying home from another show. We were also a little loud and a little loadski, which was bothering a few of the other passengers.

After a couple of complaints, a flight attendant who looked like Mrs. Garrett from *The Facts of Life* approached us in a huff.

"Gentlemen, you have to return to your seats immediately. You are far too loud and people want to sleep. As a matter of fact, the man sitting in 2D has a twenty-five-million-dollar meeting in Atlanta first thing in the morning and needs his rest!"

Hulk looked at Mrs. Garrett with a charming smile and said calmly, "If he's got a twenty-five-million-dollar meeting in the morning, why didn't he just charter a plane and sleep on that?" His logic made perfect sense to me, and I burst out laughing while Mrs. G scowled like she was Sour Boy from *Talk'n Shop*.

But we didn't want to cause any trouble, so we went back to our seats. I was planning on taking a quick nap, until suddenly I belched twice . . . and threw up on myself.

I was really surprised because I hadn't barfed from alcohol in years, especially from drinking only Yeah Boys. Upon further evaluation, I realized I hadn't thrown up too much, as there was only a silver dollar–sized dollop of bap on my right leg. I mentioned to Nash that I had just puked on myself as I cleaned it up with a napkin and some bottled water and then dozed off.

We landed in Atlanta a few hours later and I bid farewell to Big Kev, then stumbled through the terminal to the gate of my next flight with Johnny and Hulk. As I shuffled down the hallway, dragging ass from lack of sleep and too many Yeah Boys, I noticed the acidic smell of vomit wafting up to my nose. I found that a little strange, as I had already cleaned up the spew on my jeans hours earlier.

I was exhausted and collapsed into my seat on the connecting flight, ready to catch some more much needed zzzz's on the way home. So I closed my eyes and snuggled up against the window ready to enter sandman, until once again a pungent, pukey aroma assaulted my olfactory.

I opened my eyes to check out where the hell the smell was coming from, and then noticed the problem. I hadn't just regurgitated on a small section of my jeans; I had heaved all over my entire left leg. How I'd missed that I don't know, but I had been traveling for three hours with the smell of acrid smoke and up-chuck breath wafting up off my body. I had pulled the ultimate rookie faux pas by hurling on myself.

I looked across the aisle at the Hulkster and asked, "Hey, Hulk, I just realized that I have puke all over my leg. Didn't you smell it?"

"Of course I smelled it, brother. But I didn't have the heart to tell you. Plus, 'Mr. Twenty-five Million Dollar Meeting' sitting in front of you on the last flight was selling it huge and I didn't want to spoil the rib!"

The rib on who . . . Mr. Twenty-five Million Dollar Meeting, or me?

WHEN FOZZY'S *Sin and Bones* album came out in 2012, it was our biggest success up to that point chartwise, saleswise, and touringwise. As a result, we went out on tour with a laundry list of great bands from Metallica to Shinedown to Drowning Pool to Steel Panther, but the band we had the most fun with was British heavy metal legends Saxon. We had a great time touring the States on the Sacrifice and Sin tour, not only because of the chemistry between our two groups, but because of the constant barrage of insults thrown back and forth.

Led by the iconic and curmudgeonly Biff Byford, Saxon were doing their first full US tour in years and had handpicked Fozzy to open the shows. We shared a bus and a road crew, which meant we basically spent six weeks in each other's faces and got to know each other quite well. It also meant that Biff and I, the lead sing-ers and respective leaders of our bands, developed a healthy ri-valry, which led to busting each other's balls incessantly on a daily basis. I can honestly say that some of the best burns I've ever thought of in my life were directed toward the Biffster, and in turn some of the best insults I've ever received came from him.

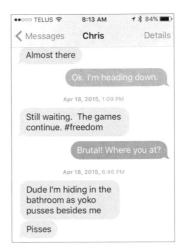

When *Metal Hammer* magazine accused Fozzy of being "heavy as lettuce," we responded by mailing them an actual head of lettuce and a lovely blue and-white-checked napkin. *(Photo by Jack Slade)*

As I crouched on the toilet seat while Yoko Ono urinated in the stall beside me at the 2015 Rock & Roll Hall of Fame ceremony, I managed to bang out this text to Wise Cousin Chad. (These are real texts btw.) *(Texts by Jericho)*

Just as this picture was taken, Gene was reacting to the news that it was Speewee's birthday. "Who gives a shit," he said . . . then stuck his tongue (apparently) down Speewee's throat. *(Photo by Paul Stanley)*

Lemmy and I salute you! Even though I've got some serious bedhead in this pic, Lem and I had a blast smoking cigs, drinking vodka, and talking rock 'n' roll all afternoon in his apartment. *(Photo by Cheryl Keuleman)*

I flew Don, Lance, and Lenny to New York City to celebrate my twenty-fifth anniversary with me. We had a blast and Lance actually laughed . . . more than once! *(Photo by random dude in the hotel lobby)*

I paid ten bucks for this piece drawn by a street artist when Lance, me, Don, and Lenny ate in a New York City diner in 2015. Hope the guy used the ten bucks on art lessons. *(Photo by Jericho)*

One of the greatest weeks of our career was playing with KISS on their Kruise in 2015. Frank was so excited, but sad that he didn't get do his Paul Stanley imitation for the Starchild. I was sad that Gene didn't fully French kiss me. *(Photo by Will Byington)*

Big Show and I realize we aren't in Kansas anymore . . . or anywhere that allows women into WWE shows. Being in Saudi Arabia made me uncomfortable. (I always forget how huge Show is until I see him standing next to me in a pic.) *(Photo by Kane)*

Frank and me with Lionel (who survived the Bataclan terrorist attack in Paris only one week earlier) in Vauréal, France. He refused to miss the Fozzy concert even though the entire country was in unrest. *(Photo by Rich Ward)*

Billy Grey and I see a mouse onstage at a Fozzy gig in Wales. *(Photo by Darren Griffiths)*

Jammin' "Beer Drinkers and Hell Raisers" with Scott Ian and Slash at Lemmy's seventieth birthday party at the Whiskey in Los Angeles. Lem passed away only a couple of weeks later. *(Photo by random rocker at the Whiskey)*

I love this pic of me and Keef. He asked me what my good side was because "I'm sixty-nine years old . . . I don't have a good side!" He also smelled really good. *(Photo by Jimmy Fallon)*

Paul and I rejoice after finding out we have no cavities at the grand opening of the Oviedo, Florida, Rock & Brews. *(Photo by Speewee)*

The team of Jericho and Styles was amazing, even if the official T-shirt was not. If you have one, in a few years it'll either be a valuable collector's item or this generation's version of a Moppy shirt. *(Photo by Xavier Woods)*

The calm before the WrestleMania storm at AT&T Stadium in Arlington . . . and in the eye of the storm only a few hours later. *(Photo courtesy of World Wrestling Entertainment, Inc.)*

Ambrose torments me in Salt Lake City, as a stupid idiot fan in the front row captures my pain. *(Photo by Stupid Idiot Fan)*

My dad hasn't quite grasped the concept of the "Selfie Stare" yet. But he's the Baby Faced Assassin, so he can do whatever the hell he wants. *(Photo by Jericho)*

Who says faces have to be in the picture for it to count as a classic shot? Sir Paul and I mimic his famous Sgt. Pepper pose and turn the backs of our heads toward the camera at the 2015 Rock & Roll Hall of Fame. *(Photo by Mr. Kite)*

Stepping out of a limo in Tokyo at 7 a.m. with a drink in hand. Well, my middle name IS Keith . . . *(Photo by Orlando Colon)*

Mike Lozanski and I conquered Monterrey, Mexico, together and were inseparable. We lived together, drank together, and wore cheesy tassled ring jackets together. I miss him. *(Photo by Corazon De Leon fan)*

Sixty-nine tacks punctured my flesh during the Asylum match . . . and it was MY choice to take the bump! What a way to make a living. *(Photo courtesy of World Wrestling Entertainment, Inc.)*

After a picture of the tack bump went viral, dozens of hilarious Photoshopped memes appeared online, including the "Creation of the Tack Bump" and "The Fifth Beatle." *(Memes by creative Friends of Jericho)*

With my beautiful family snorkeling in Maui. Jessica, Cheyenne, Ash, Sierra, and I enjoyed Shep Gordon's hospitality to the max, and we will never forget him or his wonderful assistant Nancy Meola. "Aloha, Shep!" *(Photo by snorkel boat captain)*

Scarves, vests, and clipboards . . . I'm at the point in my career where I have the confidence to take a chance and get almost anything over. Which is a good thing, because I'd look absolutely ridiculous if I didn't! *(Photo courtesy of World Wrestling Entertainment, Inc.)*

You'll believe a man can fly . . . or at least jump off a twenty-foot steel cage at forty-three years old. I'd do it today too if it made for a better match. *(Photo courtesy of World Wrestling Entertainment, Inc.)*

Here's the move that I single-handedly got unbanned by Vince McMahon. Funny thing is, it's so easy to take and gets such a great reaction that I'd take it every night if I had to. *(Photo courtesy of World Wrestling Entertainment, Inc.*

I would wake up each morning and say to Biff with surprise, "Wow, you're still alive? You know people of your advanced age (he was sixty-two) die in their sleep all the time."

He could give as good as he got, however, and justified the substantial number of fans who attended Fozzy's VIP meet and greets by saying they were all wrestling fans who could care less about the "wank music of Fozzy." I would then point out Fozzy's pretty female fans in the crowd and explain to him that they were called "girls," something that Saxon rarely had in their audiences, which were made up primarily of denim-and-leather-wearing dudes.

The rivalry got more serious at the House of Blues in Dallas, when Biff informed me that we weren't allowed to use the venue's entire lighting rig during our show because that was reserved for the headliner.

"No problem, Biff. As a matter of fact, you can turn off ALL the lights if you want. We'll play in total darkness and still blow your band away."

We argued about everything and no topic was off limits. But nothing caused as much controversy between us as THE CHICKEN.

Yes, Constant Reader . . . THE CHICKEN. A subject so hotly debated that it still elicits laughter from every member of Fozzy whenever somebody brings it up. We've even written a rap song about it that goes something like this:

Where's my chicken?
I want chicken!
I love chicken!
Give me chicken . . .

How did this flavorsome fowl become such a contentious topic you might ask? Well, it started early in the tour when Biff happened to walk into our dressing room and saw our rider on the table. A band's rider usually includes fresh fruit, a deli tray, potato chips, various chocolates, soft drinks, etc. However, Fozzy's rider stipulates that along with all of that stuff, there must also be a roasted chicken in our dressing room at every show. That's a little unusual, I'll grant you, but I made sure to include THE CHICKEN on the rider, to make sure that we got at least one healthy meal during the day.

It must've been a good idea, because band after band from Steel Panther to Slash's Conspirators have followed my lead and included one on their riders after touring with us. Why Biff, who'd been touring since the Dark Ages, had never thought of adding THE CHICKEN to his rider I don't know, but he was not happy that Fozzy had one and Saxon didn't.

"Why do you have a chicken, Jericho?"

"Because I asked for one, Biff."

"Where's my chicken?"

"Did you ask for one?"

"No."

"Well, that's why you don't have one. Now get the hell out of our dressing room, you old fuck."

Moments later, I heard him berating his tour manager for not getting him a chicken. Even though he had one the next night, he must've kept forgetting to include it on Saxon's official rider, because he would constantly grumble, "There's Fozzy's fuckin' chicken again" or "Well, why does Fozzy get a fuckin' chicken and we don't?"

Biff's bitterness over THE CHICKEN became a running joke and was a constant laugh for us that helped make the tour go by quicker. But after six weeks of being together constantly, Biff and I needed a break from each other, and I was happy when we got to the final show at the Venue in Vancouver. However, after such a successful run, I wanted to make sure that Biff and his guys had a proper sendoff back to the UK.

So I asked our tour manager to buy five roast chickens and five silver platters and bring them into our dressing room during

Saxon's set. We grabbed the perky poultry, put them on the silver platters, and waited for the right moment to strike.

Saxon tore the house down that night as they always did (they're one of the best live bands I've ever seen), and the crowd was going nuts as they winded their way towards the end of their set with a rousing rendition of one of their biggest songs, "Wheels of Steel."

Every night they broke it down and led the crowd in a massive "Wheels of Steel" chant, and that was going to be our cue. When the sing-along started, we grabbed our silver platters and ambled onstage to serve Biff his much desired CHICKENS.

They had no idea the gag was coming, and when they saw us walk onstage, they burst out laughing (but didn't miss a beat) as we fed them various wings, drum sticks, and breasts. Biff stared at me with a "you little shit" look on his face, but I could tell he thought it was pretty funny. After the band had eaten their fill, we threw the rest of the tasty bird into the audience so the fans could enjoy a snack as well.

It was an awesome moment, and if you were there that night in Vancouver, feel free to hit me up on the twittah at @iamjericho and let me know if you were able to grab a piece of THE CHICKEN!

After the show Biff said, "That was a good one, you wanker. I was going to buy a couple of electric fans, tear open some pillows, and blow the feathers at you from the side of the stage during your set."

"But you didn't, Biff!"

"Yeah, I decided I didn't want to torture myself by sitting through your whole show."

Well played, Biff! Treat yourself to a CHICKEN on me.

THINKING ABOUT the Saxon rib still makes me smile and is a perfect example of going the extra mile to make an experience more memorable whenever you can. You won't regret it . . . and it always makes for a better story.

My Wise Cousin Chad and I have made it a tradition to attend the annual Rock & Roll Hall of Fame inductions. We're obsessed with music, and thanks to meeting the amazing Betsy Hill of *Rolling Stone* magazine at our first ceremony, we have the ultimate connection to hook us up.

In 2015, it was announced that Ringo Starr was finally being honored by the Hall as a solo act and would be inducted by his old bandmate Paul McCartney. Wise Cousin Chad and I were stoked, because we have been huge Beatles fans since we first got into them at the same time in the early '80s.

The show was in Cleveland that year, and Betsy was able to get us arena floor passes, which was awesome because that's where all the inductees and VIPs sat. The only catch was we didn't have an actual seat at any of the tables, so even though security couldn't kick us out, we didn't have anywhere specific to go. So our plan was to roam around the floor and stay out of everybody's way. But if we stood at one spot for too long, security would tell us to move, and we would simply wander to the other side of the venue. Because of Ringo's induction, musical royalty were everywhere. I literally bumped into Stevie Wonder and Sting, Bruce Springsteen, John Legend, and my buds Alice Cooper and Dave Grohl walked by us at various times. Joan Jett was the first to get inducted, followed by Lou Reed and then the Five Royales. As each act was honored, I noticed Paul and Ringo with their wives sitting at a table at the front of the venue, along with Olivia Harrison and Yoko Ono. As is custom, whenever an act was inducted they would play a short set of their biggest hits, or another artist would play a few songs in tribute to them. At that point, the entire crowd would stand up, cheer along, and watch the artists rock, so nobody really knew who was sitting where. I decided that's when I would make my move.

I'd been waiting my whole life to meet Paul and had tried several times at his gigs over the years, but had been shut down by security every time. However, tonight I had my chance.

When Green Day was inducted, everyone gave them a stand-ing ovation as they began to play. I'd never seen them before and they were incredible, full of energy, and had great crowd par-ticipation. It was the perfect time for Wise Cousin Chad and me to make our way up to the front of the arena unnoticed, so we pushed our way through the crowd and situated ourselves at a table directly behind the Fab Two. We gave a friendly greeting to the other people at the table, like we had been sitting there all night and they grinned back, having no idea that we didn't belong there. I didn't care if they did anyway, because we were Beatle hunting and that was serious business.

As I watched the bobbing mopheads in front of me, I couldn't believe I was standing only a few feet from the two biggest rock stars on the planet, legends whose band had influenced me and the world more than any other. Their silhouettes walking across Abbey Road were even tattooed on my left arm. It was a surreal experience, especially seeing Paul rocking out to Green Day when they performed "American Idiot." During the song, Billie Joe Armstrong led the crowd in a rousing "HEY!" between the main riff, and Paul seemed to be screaming the loudest, throw-ing his fist up in the air with every shout.

Finally, Green Day finished their short albeit powerful set and Macca got up to leave the table with his security guard following closely behind. I assumed he was going to the loo, so I decided to follow. To not be so obvious, I walked down a different row of tables than they did, leading to a fork in the furniture road, where Paul and I ended up face to face. I'd been waiting for this moment my whole life and knew I only had a few seconds to make a good impression before the bathroom window closed, so I opened with my best line.

"Hey, Paul, I saw you rocking to Green Day. They were pretty damn good, huh?"

Not a bad start. I didn't want to pull the old "thank you so much for the music" fanboy speech like I did when I first met

James Hetfield. I knew nothing would get me on the "creepy fanatic" radar quicker than that line of conversation.

Paul looked at me and replied good naturedly in his Liverpool lilt, "Yeah, they were pretty fookin' good, man."

Okay, that was encouraging. I'd gotten a response from him on a dude level, not a "go away stalker" level. Now it was time to unleash some witty repartee and show him I was a hilarious cat worthy of hanging out with.

"Hey, man, I see you have your security in front of you. Just want to let you know that I'll be your backline security if you want . . . you know, in case any ninjas try to attack you."

Paul looked at me quizzically.

"Ninjas? Okay, I'll keep that in mind."

Then he turned to walk away. Even though I hadn't received an offer to spend the night at his house or gotten his email address, I'd still had a conversation with PAUL McCARTNEY and I thought that was pretty gear. Mission accomplished!

But I wanted more and couldn't contain myself, so I finally unfurled my fanboy freak flag, threw my arm in the air and blurted out, "Hey, Paul . . . HIGH FIVE!"

Paul glanced up at my raised palm, and to his credit decided not to leave me hanging. He gamely slapped my hand and walked off to piss.

I couldn't believe what had happened. I'd taken a chance to meet Paul and it worked! Wise Cousin Chad and I shared a high five of our own and squealed like a couple of Apple Scruffs in 1968.

We decided to hit the bathroom before grabbing another cocktail from the friendly waitress who had taken pity on us for having no particular place to go. She'd been quite gracious with the Yeah Boys, and we were pretty buzzed by the time we got to the canski. It was a big lavatory with two sections, the first equipped with sinks and urinals, and the second boasting a row of stalls and more basins. The pissers were all occupied, so I went around the corner and was waiting in line, when an official-looking guy wearing a suit with an official-looking laminate hanging around his neck stomped over.

"Everybody needs to clear the bathroom. I've got Yoko coming in."

The other guys in the biffy chuckled, but Suit-and-Tie Guy wasn't laughing.

"I'm serious, Yoko is coming in here so everybody has to leave."

There was no doubt that this guy was serious, so everybody followed his directions and got out of the bathroom.

Everybody that is, except for me.

The washroom cleared out fast, leaving me completely alone in the room. So in the fine tradition of having a good time all the time, I decided to stick around . . . inside one of the stalls.

There were three of them lined up in the bathroom, so I chose the middle one. I went inside, locked the door, and then crouched down on the edge of the commode like a teenage camper hiding from Jason Voorhees in a *Friday the 13th* movie. I'm not sure what my plan was, but it seemed like a good idea at the time, until I started thinking about what I would do if she decided she wanted to use the middle biffy.

I waited for a few minutes until I heard the distinct Japanese accent of Yoko Ono. She was with another lady, and why wouldn't she be? I mean even Yoko goes to the bathroom with a friend, right? The bad news was my chances of being busted in the middle cubicle had just doubled.

I crouched on the stall helplessly waiting to be exposed, but then the hand of outhouse fate stepped in.

"I'll go in this one," Yoko said, and went into the toilet on my left. Her friend must've wanted a little buffer, so she went into the one on my right, and I thanked Lucy in the sky with diamonds that I'd been left undetected.

I waited in silence, wondering what was going to happen next, when I heard the distinct sound of cloth being pulled across skin. Then I saw a corner of the black dress she was wearing slide under the wall of the cubicle and heard the faint tinkling sound of liquid hitting the toilet water.

I got out my phone and texted Wise Cousin Chad discreetly—DUDE, I'M HIDING IN THE BATHROOM AS YOKO PISSES BESIDES ME!—as the sound of Yoko's flow permeated my ears.

Now, let me take a moment to say there's no question that my actions were incredibly creepy and totally invasive to Ms. Ono's privacy. But the whole thing is also pretty fuckin' funny and makes for an amazing story, so I accept and own said criticism. Now back to our story.

After a few seconds, the piece of black dress disappeared back under the stall and I heard Yoko stand up and flush. She unlocked the door and walked out of the potty. This was my cue.

I stepped off the throne, unlocked the door, and came face to face with Yoko Ono. I couldn't believe how tiny she was, but her presence was huge as she gazed at me stoically. I raised my hands and looked around confusedly.

"Oh my goodness. I am SO sorry! I thought this was the boys' bathroom!?"

"It is the boys' bathroom. I was just using it," she said looking over the rims of her prominently placed sunglasses.

"Well, I'm sorry for interrupting you, Yoko."

"It's okay," she said softly, and walked over to the sink.

I felt weird and I wasn't sure if she believed me or not, but I don't blame her if she didn't. I'm sure stupid idiots like me pull this type of shit on her all the time and she deals with crazy fans on a daily basis. But even though I might've been crazy, I wasn't a filthy animal and still wanted to wash my hands, so I sidled up at the sink next to hers. She glanced over and smiled as I turned on the faucet, and I couldn't believe how surprisingly pleasant she was under the circumstances.

"Are you having a fun night, Yoko?"

"Oh yes. So nice to see everybody."

I soaped up and washed the lather off my hands under the lukewarm water from the tap. When I was done, I turned the faucet off and shook my hands to get rid of the residual drops. Then I looked around and noticed that all of the paper towel receptacles were empty. At this point one, of the security guards came in with a stack of napkins and gave them to Yoko.

As she dried off her hands, she noticed I was towelless and offered her stack of serviettes to me.

"Here, take one of these. You can't leave with wet hands."

I was touched by her offer to spare a square.

"Thank you so much, Yoko," I said as I grabbed a napkin and dried my hands off. "I hope you have a great night!"

"Thank you," she replied, and was shuffled off by her handlers, the biggest of which stared at me like he wanted to rip my clean hands clean off.

"Wow . . . I have no idea what just happened!" I declared to the guy in amazement and brushed past him out the door.

Wise Cousin Chad was waiting outside and burst out in laughter when I told him what happened. Once again, I know it was a creepy thing to do, but it made for the tale of a lifetime (and a great chapter for this book) and therefore was worth it. However, I would like to officially apologize to Yoko for invading her privacy and thank her for being so gracious to me, even though I'm quite sure she knew I was full of shit . . . or pee in this case.

The night progressed and we decided to go straight to the front row for Ringo's speech and the subsequent mini-concert, where he played his biggest hits with Paul, Joe Walsh, Paul Shaffer, Joan Jett, and the Green Day guys. If you ever see the telecast on HBO, you might notice a guy who keeps blocking McCartney's face on the hard camera shot by waving his tattooed arms in the air like he just don't care. Constant Reader . . . of course that was me.

When the ceremony was over, Betsy got Wise Cousin Chad and me passes to the exclusive *Rolling Stone* after-party, which once again was packed with dignitaries. I had great conversations with Billie Joe from Green Day (a Fozzy fan who'd enjoyed watching Rich and me on a recent episode of VH-1's *That Metal*

Show) and Paul Shaffer, with whom I'd been on the Jimmy Fallon show a few years prior. We also witnessed poor Robbie Robertson sitting in a booth talking to himself, saw drummer Anton Fig literally eating a fig, and gave our favorite fashion designer, John Varvatos, some sage advice.

"Please don't ever go out of business," Wise Cousin Chad stammered as John nodded and took notes. But the biggest star of them all was once again only a few feet away. I noticed Paul having a drink with his wife and Joe Walsh in the booth next to us. People were approaching him and asking for autographs and pictures, but after already having my McCartney moment earlier in the night, I didn't want to bother him any further. Plus, after hearing him mention on Chris Hardwick's podcast (curse you for getting him, Hardwick!) that he loved talking to fans but felt very uncomfortable when they asked for a picture, because at that point he ceased being Paul and turned into "That Famous Guy."

With those words in mind, I was happy just hanging around his general vicinity and drinking in the froot vibes he was sending out. However, when he got up to get some food he was surrounded again, so I decided to extend an offer of help.

"Hey, Paul," I approached and said, "if you're getting bothered too much, just let me know and I'll clear everybody out of the way."

Confused by my offer, Paul looked up at me and a flicker of recognition crossed his face. I could tell he remembered me from earlier! I was on cloud #9, because this was the part when he was going to say he watched me on TV and was a big fan of my work. Then he would give me his cell phone number, follow me on Twitter, like me on Facebook, and become my new best friend! (Sorry, Kevin Owens.)

Paul opened his mouth, and as I prepared to accept his invitation to go on tour with him, he threw me a curve ball.

"Who ARE you, man?"

Hmmm . . . that wasn't what I was expecting. But maybe I hadn't heard him correctly.

"Who ARE you, man?" (nope . . . I'd heard him) he repeated with his whimsical accent. "I saw you before . . . are you a security guard or a cameraman?"

A cameraman? Did he think I worked for TMZ or some shit? I stood there trying to think of another witty response, but before I could stammer anything out, Paul cut me off.

"Listen, man, if I need any help with the ninjas or anybody else, I'll let you know, okay mate?"

He gave me a thumbs-up and turned away. I was happy he remembered my ninja comment, but I smelled what he was cooking. He was friendly with his tone, but his overall message was "You're starting to creep me out, dude, so please leave me alone."

I don't blame him for feeling a weird vibe about me . . . after all, I had just hid in a toilet stall and listened to his late best friend's wife take a leak.

CHAPTER 10

THE
TWELFTH
NINJA
PRINCIPLE

ENJOY THE MOMENT

I know I know for sure,
that life is beautiful around the world . . .
—RED HOT CHILI PEPPERS, "AROUND THE WORLD"

When Vanilla Ice guested on *Talk Is Jericho*, I found him to be a friendly, humble, and inspiring guy who realized it was an honor to be able to survive and prosper in show business for over twenty-five years. After years of being embarrassed by the monster success of "Ice Ice Baby," he had recently embraced it and as a result, was enjoying a massive resurgence both as a musician and as a TV star after he REINVENTED (see chapter 20) himself as a home renovation expert. We had a great chat in one of the homes he had fixed up for *The Vanilla Ice Project*, his home improvement show on the DIY Network, and during our interview he passed on a great piece of advice from an eighty-five-year-old friend of his, whom he'd nicknamed "The Twelfth Ninja."

"Slow down, don't stress, and enjoy what you have. Because in the end, you're gonna end up old just like me anyway."

That wise ninja was right.

I find that life moves so fast, with so much going on at all times that it's easy to forget to enjoy the fruits of your labors and savor the successes along the way. The problem with being on a Fozzy tour or working a full WWE schedule is that there's always another match or concert just a few hundred miles down the road, so one tends to bleed into the other. But that's no excuse not to take a moment for yourself to enjoy the experience . . . to drink it in, maaan.

Around 2002, right as The Rock left the WWE to become a worldwide movie star, he told me, "Appreciate every match you have. At some point, it's going to be your last one and you won't believe how fast it's all gone. Take a moment for yourself and take a look at the crowd. Enjoy their reactions. Because when it's time for it to end, you're going to miss it. I know I already do."

I took his advice and always take a few seconds after a match to stand at the top of the stage and experience the moment, because I don't know when I'll be back in that city again.

It's like Ferris Bueller said, "Life moves pretty fast. If you don't stop and look around once in a while, you could miss it."

Truer words were never spoken.

I encourage everyone reading to listen to the Sausage King of Chicago and take a look around sometimes. It sounds a little clichéd, but I'm telling you there is some truth here: live in the moment, smell the metaphorical roses, and don't just rush on to the next appointment or goal in your life. This is even truer after a victory or a success. Don't forget to acknowledge all the hard work you've put in, or more importantly, the people who've helped you along the way, especially your family.

I couldn't have accomplished all the things I have without the support of my incredible and beautiful wife, Jessica. She's my rock and supports me through all the ups and downs of my career and my life. Every success I have is a shared victory, and without her love and advice I wouldn't be as driven or as bold with my decisions. I also have three amazing children who are my raison d'être and drive me to be the best that I can be in whatever I do. It's a huge sacrifice to be away from Ash, Cheyenne, and Sierra for weeks at a time sometimes, so if I am going to pay that stiff price, I won't accept anything less than performing at my absolute best when I'm on the road . . . I owe that to them and their love pulls me through.

But when all of the hard work causes everything to line up and you hit the jackpot, it makes all of the sacrifices worthwhile. That's why you owe it to yourself to count those proverbial tokens coming out of the machine, listen to the jingling sounds they make as they fill up that plastic cup, and savor the thrill of your victories.

After every performance, I'm always the last guy in the dressing room, as I like to sit there and reflect upon the night. The late Roddy Piper once told me that being a main eventer was the loneliest position in the company because by the time you've finished your match and get back to the dressing room, everybody else is gone. He was right, but I never had a problem being by myself after the show. I like relaxing and analyzing that night's performance while listening to tunes, changing out of my sweaty clothes, and having a drink. One of my favorite things to do after Fozzy gigs is to hang around with our drummer, Frank Fontsere, and talk about music and life. Make sure to take that time to celebrate your success. You work too hard not to!

In 2016, we had the biggest WrestleMania of all time in front of over a hundred thousand people at AT&T Stadium in Arlington, Texas. Now, I've worked over a dozen stadium shows in my career, but I never take it for granted when I have the honor of performing in such a giant venue in front of a massive, enthused crowd. So a few hours before the show began, I made my customary pilgrimage to the top of the massive WrestleMania stage and wandered back and forth from one side of the gargantuan structure to the other, surveying the thousands of empty seats in front of me. It was a kind of WrestleMania tradition for me, as it helped clear my head and gave me the chance to reflect on how much I'd been through on my way back to that grand stage.

As I was drinking it in before Mania 32, I saw Vince walk onstage to survey the Brobdingnagian box of Booty-O's that was to be the centerpiece of The New Day's entrance. They were rehearsing the tipping of the box where random Booty-O's would scatter across the stage, revealing the hugely popular trio.

I walked over to Vince and said, "Wow, the biggest WrestleMania of all time, eh?"

"It's incredible, right?" he answered. "Over a hundred thousand people will be here in just a few hours."

I smiled and said, "You've come a long way since New Haven, kid."

Vince grinned and swatted me away with his rundown sheet, laughing at the fact that I knew New Haven was the first arena his father had allowed him to promote in the mid-'70s. As I walked back down the ramp, I glanced over my shoulder and saw Vince looking out at the empty stadium with a satisfied look on his face. There was no doubt in my mind that he was enjoying the moment, and that made me happy.

WrestleMania is a once-a-year milestone that's revered by everyone in the WWE, and the biggest show of the year for the company. It's very special to me as well, but there's another annual occasion that personally is more important, and that's October 2, the date of my very first match in 1990. You need to appreciate those personal milestones in your own life, and I have honored this one since October 2, 1995, my fifth anniversary in the wrestling business. I was on tour for WAR in Japan with Los

Brazos, a trio of *luchador* brothers I'd met while working in Mexico, and when they found out that my debut match was exactly five years earlier, they bought me a cake to celebrate.

"Don't ever forget these special days, my friend. Every year that you continue to do what you love is a blessing," said El Brazo, the middle brother.

I've never forgotten what he told me, and every year on October 2 I say a prayer thanking the Lord for allowing me to continue to do what I love to do, whether I'm currently wrestling in the WWE or not. In 2015, I was working with the company and coincidentally a Madison Square Garden date had been booked on October 3, which was exactly the twenty-fifth anniversary (plus one day) of my first match. I decided I wanted to do something extra special to commemorate my silver anniversary on the job, and share the date with the guys who were there with me at the beginning.

I called Lance Storm, "Dr. Luther" Lenny St. Claire, Don Callis, and Brett Como, inviting all of them to fly to New York City to hang for a couple of days and go to the show. I wanted to give them a small token of appreciation to let them know how much their friendship meant to me, both in the early days and now.

With the exception of Como, everybody was able to make it, and from the moment we saw each other again (even though we hadn't been in the same room together for over twenty years), it was like not a minute had passed. The true brothers you meet in the business and spend so much time with on the road are like war buddies—guys you fought with in the trenches that you have a special bond with that lasts forever. Whenever you see them, even if it's been a long period of time, you pick up right where you left off . . . which usually means busting each other's balls incessantly.

Callis immediately complained that I hadn't flown him first class, while Lenny and I slipped right into our old made-up road characters we had invented in the mid-'90s, and Lance cracked a smile . . . once.

We went to a late-night diner to catch up, and as we were sitting around laughing, a street "artist" drew the absolute worst picture of us that you could imagine. We gave the guy ten bucks for it anyway, as we had to have the picture and couldn't let such a hideous effort go unrewarded. The guys then presented me with a mock old-school wrestling poster featuring old promo pictures of the four of us from the early '90s. It was the most amazing gift they could've given me and I loved it, although I'm not exactly sure where I put it. It's in my house somewhere! In return, I gave them each a special "Y25J" commemorative twenty-fifth anniversary T-shirt that the WWE was selling for one night only at MSG.

The next night at the show, WWE.com interviewed all three of them and gave them a nice rub by putting an extensive article up on the website detailing where their various careers had led them over the years. We took pictures backstage together, which was especially cool and personally significant for Lenny, who had never been to MSG before, and Don, who had made his WWE debut there as The Jackal almost twenty years prior.

When I had mentioned my twenty-fifth anniversary plans to Vince a few months earlier, he loved the idea and insisted that the guys sit at the timekeepers' table, but the night of the show he wanted to have them sit in the front row instead. The decision had been made to make the show a live WWE Network special, which meant time constraints on my match with Kevin Owens. But I still wanted to cut a pre-match promo and figured after twenty-five years on the job, if I wanted some time to address the crowd, I should get it. I wanted to enjoy the moment of such an important occasion (how many guys stay successful in the wrestling business for twenty-five years?) and share some of my MSG memories with some of the greatest Jerichoholics in the world.

I started the promo by pointing up into the stands where I was sitting as a four-year-old kid when I got mad at my dad for not waving to me when he was on a breakaway as a New York Ranger.

Then I pointed out my three friends in the front row and gave them each a shout out, thanking them for all they had done for me throughout my career. I told a few other anecdotes and threw out a couple Jericho classic catchphrases before finishing up, so Owens and I could start our match. The promo went long, which cut our match down to about twelve minutes, but we made the most of it and had a pretty damn good match, which of course I lost. It was the right finish, as twenty-fifth anniversary or not, I still had a responsibility to do what was best for business. But it was an amazing way to celebrate my quarter-century jubilee, and the night was just beginning.

I had received an invite from Benjamin Steak House, one of the best in New York City, to celebrate the occasion with my pals, gratis. We had an outstanding meal and I looked like a real big shot when the check came and everything was on the house (Callis finally stopped bitching about not flying first class). Then we went back to the five-star hotel I had booked us in and re-corded the "Jericho 25th Anniversary" episode of *Talk Is Jericho*, which ended up being one of the funniest in the show's history. The laughs began right off the bat, when I pulled a desk back from the wall to access the electrical outlet and found a condom wrapper and a Yankees ticket stub from three years prior. Five-star hotel indeed!

It was the perfect starting point for ninety minutes of pure ridiculousness that ended up with Lance collapsing on the floor from a laughing fit. Storm isn't exactly known for his chuckling skills, but he sure as hell let loose that night. He was literally rolling around on the ground, unable to stop as the tears poured from his eyes for such a long time I was able to take a dozen pic-tures for proof. If you haven't heard that podcast, you need to go online and check it out. If you don't find it funny, I'll personally give you your money back, even though it's free.

As much fun as we had, my favorite part of the whole week-end was reconnecting with my old friends, who admittedly I should've kept in better contact with over the years. But spending those few days with my bros helped me remember how close we were and how deep our connection would always be. Now I text with all three guys almost daily and we are closer than ever. The whole twenty-fifth anniversary experience was the perfect example of taking extra measures to relish the moment, to appreciate life, and to thank lifelong friends for all they'd done along the way.

In closing, I'll see you all at Madison Square Garden on October 3, 2040, for the Jericho fiftieth anniversary celebration. Maybe I'll even hold a contest to see which one of you lucky Friends of Jericho gets to wheel me to the ring.

CHAPTER 11

THE GROUNDLINGS PRINCIPLE

ALWAYS COMMIT

Who can go the distance,
we'll find out in the long run . . .
—EAGLES, "THE LONG RUN"

I walked away from the WWE for the first time in August of 2005, because I was burned out and had no interest in working in the wrestling business anymore. It was a scary time for me, a kind of "midlife career crisis" if you wheeel, as I was uncertain of where the future was going to take me. In retrospect, taking a break from the company was the best decision I could have ever made, because those twenty-seven months away from wrestling not only gave me the chance to realize how much I wanted to be in the WWE, but they also gave me the opportunity to expand my horizons. I learned some very important additional skills during that time, which I used to become a better performer in the long run (and I ain't talkin' bout Joe Walsh).

One of the main lessons I learned from working with the famed Los Angeles improv comedy troupe the Groundlings was to "always commit." In improv, always committing means that no matter how ridiculous the situation is onstage, you give it a hundred percent to make it as real and funny to the audience as possible. If you are supposed to be a giant duck delivering pizzas to Lady Gaga and you show any hesitation with your performance, the audience can smell that from a mile away and you'll bomb. In other words, if you don't buy what you're selling, why would anybody else?

That mindset doesn't just apply to improv, Constant Reader. It can and should be used in all aspects of your life. In the classic words of my boy Hurricane Helms, "If you ain't in, then you must be out!"

The idea of always committing is an offshoot of the "Believe in Yourself" mantra that we've been talking about throughout this entire tome, but this goes a step further: always committing also means making a promise to yourself. An oath that you'll follow through no matter how hard things get, without compromise. It's not easy to do, but I promise you that if you always commit, you'll eventually get what you want.

The biggest and most prestigious annual heavy metal festival in the world is Germany's Wacken (pronounced "Vacken"), and Fozzy had been trying without success to get booked there since we started in 2000. At first I think it was because the organizers thought we were just a "novelty" band, but when we released our first all-original album, *All That Remains,* in 2005, they finally showed a little interest in booking us, but with a catch: they wanted me to wrestle as well.

Every year, besides having over a hundred bands play, the Wacken festival includes carnival rides, tattooing, face painting, and . . . a live wrestling show for which the promoters wanted to book me on in exchange for using Fozzy.

I realized early on in Fozztory that it was best for the band and myself to keep the church and state of rock 'n' roll and wrestling separate. It was hard enough for us to gain respect as a legitimate kickass rock band in the early years solely because I was the singer. A lot of people assumed that because I was a celebrity from another field that Fozzy was just a vanity project and couldn't possibly be any good. In some ways I don't blame them, as there had been enough Dogstars, Wicked Worlds, and the Return of Brunos for haters to compare us to.

But as we matured over the years, and it became apparent that we could blow a lot of other groups off the stage, I knew we had a real chance to get to the next level. I believed the best way to do that would be to keep a division between my two careers: to show people we were in this to rock the world, not to rock my ego. Therefore, I felt that if I acquiesced to Wacken's request to work double duty, it would be the equivalent of Taylor Momsen delivering a Cindy Lou Who monologue before a Pretty Reckless set just because she was in *How the Grinch Stole Christmas* when she was seven.

I told our manager, Mark Willis, to turn them down unless it was for Fozzy only. He was more than happy to do so, and we were excluded from the bill for yet another year.

When *Chasing the Grail* came out in 2010, we got another offer from Wacken with a better slot on the bill and an additional five thousand dollars if I would lace up the boots and get in the ring. Now don't get me wrong, five grand is a nice chunk of change, and way more than I would make for a WWE live event in Asheville, North Carolina, on a Sunday afternoon, but that wasn't the point. We had told the festival organizers that Fozzy would be happy to come to Germany and kick everybody's asses, but we weren't interested in me wrestling as well. So once again the answer was no.

We were fine with it, though this had gone beyond just playing the festival; it had become a war of attrition between us and the promoters. They knew the terms we had given them to appear on the festival, yet they kept trying to con us into doing it their way regardless. Also, we had already played Download (along with most of the other big festivals in the UK) multiple times, and they hadn't asked us for anything more than to put on a killer show, so we felt like the precedent had been set: we were a damn good rock 'n' roll band and should be treated as such. It's not like they asked Rob Zombie to hang out in the field and operate the Ferris wheel before his set, so why did I have to wrestle before we played ours?

When we released *Sin and Bones* in 2012, once again Wacken wanted me to wrestle, and once again I said absolutely not. The organizers were baffled, and I felt at this point that we had worn out our *willkommen*. It was a drag, but I still believed that if we stuck to our guns, we would get our chance to play Wacken someday on our own damn terms.

Lo and behold, I was right.

As fate would have it, we were booked at Download that year for the second time, this time on the bigger second stage, and drew a ridiculous crowd of over twenty thousand Fozzy fanatics at the ungodly hour (at least for a rock show) of 12:30 p.m. We played one of the best shows of our career, and plenty of heavy hitters in the industry were there to take notice, including a bigwig talent booker who represented . . . you guessed it . . . Wacken.

He was so impressed with our music and stage presence that it wasn't long after that we got an offer to play the following year's Wacken festival, with a good guarantee, good stage positioning, and most importantly, no wrestling required.

By committing to our vision of who we were as a band and refusing to compromise said vision, we got what we wanted and then some. We had an awesome Wacken debut, in front of a great crowd of eight thousand who showed up even though we were clashing with Alice Cooper, who was playing on the main stage right beside us. The crowd went so nuts for us that three of our songs were included on the live video compilation of the festival, even though most of the other bands only had two.

Don't get me wrong. I know that it's hard to stay committed to your beliefs at times, especially when there's a nice paycheck being dangled in front of your face, but that's nothing compared to the difficulties of staying dedicated to the cause when your professional reputation is in question.

When I came back to the WWE in January 2016 after another fifteen-month hiatus from television, the plan was for me to eventually turn heel. I'd been a babyface for the last three-odd years, but with my frequent breaks away from the company, it seemed that each return brought me one step closer to overstaying my welcome with the fans. Plus, my Y2J act was getting stale and there was only so much more I could do in that role, so I knew the time was ripe to turn heel again.

I was actually looking forward to it, as there's a certain comfort level I have as a heel that I don't have when I'm a good guy. Case in point, I'm a six-time WWE world champion and every one of those has been as a heel. So with that in mind, I was excited to get back to doing what I do best . . . pissing people off.

The original idea was for me to turn right after the Royal Rumble, but then I started working with AJ Styles and Vince decided to stretch out our program for a few more months. He wanted me to stay babyface a little longer as a result, but even though my turn wasn't imminent, I started doing subtle things to annoy the fans and plant the seeds for the heel turn that was coming up around the bend.

The first step was simple: stop wearing a shirt.

I'd walk to the ring wearing a blazer with nothing underneath or a vest with tight jeans and boots. I have no idea why this rubbed people the wrong way, but I started getting dozens of tweets daily with comments like CAN'T JERICHO AFFORD ANY CLOTHES? or I'M BEGGING JERICHO TO PUT ON A SHIRT. Those kinds of responses showed me I was getting under people's skin, which theoretically isn't a good thing when you're supposed to be a babyface, but in the big picture was perfect. Then I added a scarf to the ensemble, and judging by the outraged reaction it received, you would've thought I was wearing a bra and panties made of baby-seal skin to the ring.

I never would've guessed how much controversy a simple piece of fancy fabric wrapped around my neck could cause, and I received more negative feedback about that thing on a daily basis from the moment I started wearing it. The scarf has even become a staple of my act on live events, when I refuse to take it off until my opponent takes it off me, to the delight of the fans. It's quite the crowd pleaser when Finn Balor or Roman Reigns prance around the ring wearing my stolen scarf, then take it off and blow their nose with it. Not fair, I say!

After the dodgy wardrobe choices, the next step to making sure people continued getting sick of me was shoving the stale elements of babyface Jericho down their throats. For example, overusing the catchphrases I'd been spouting since the George W. Bush administration worked like a charm.

Every week I would stand in the middle of the ring on *Raw* and say, "Welcome to *Raw Is Jericho!*" or "Would You Please Shut the Hell Up!" and of course, "You Will Never EEEVVVEEERRR Be the Same Again."

All of those were top-ten hits on the WWE catchphrase charts fifteen years ago, but lamely spouting them out ad nauseam in the modern era made me seem flat and out of touch. Once again I started getting a ton of negative feedback echoing that sentiment, which to me was a double-edged sword. On one hand, it was cool to know that my plan was working, but on the other hand, it was hard to not scream from the rooftops that I wasn't actually out of touch, but rather I knew exactly what I was doing! I was working everybody with my true commitment.

The night I returned to *Raw* in San Antonio in January 2016, I was involved in a segment with The New Day, one of the freshest acts to grace the WWE in a long time. I took extra pride when they started their rise to popularity, as I had predicted they would be big a year earlier and even had them on *Talk Is Jericho* when they were still a prelim act. Big E, Xavier Woods, and my old rival Kofi Kingston were hip, contemporary, funny, and had chemistry coming out of their Booty-O's, so I was excited to be working with them.

When you're dealing with an act as unique as New Day, who had gotten toy unicorn horns, a trombone, and a box of cereal over, you had to play along with them. I couldn't go out there and no-sell their goofiness or try to be über-serious, because that would ignore what had gotten them over and essentially bury them.

I had to play along with their quirkiness, so I came up with the idea of calling them "Rooty Tooty Booty," which doesn't make sense and if we're calling an ace of spades an ace of spades, is really fuckin stupid.

But the kicker is, I knew it was stupid.

It might have gotten over huge in the salad days of the Attitude Era, when fans were chanting whatever I wanted them to ("filthy, dirty, disgusting, brutal, bottom-feeding trash bag ho" comes to mind), but this one wasn't getting much traction. Was it painful to lead a "Rooty Tooty Booty" chant with only 20 percent of the audience joining in? Of course it was, but that was the price I had to pay to keep the facade of my out-of-touch, slightly annoying character rolling.

Eventually, "Rooty Tooty Booty" died a much-deserved death, and I ended up turning heel on AJ Styles after a classic tag team title match with The New Day in Chicago. Suddenly, my character was rejuvenated, and on the strength of great matches and a slew of surprise late-career hit catchphrases like "Stupid Idiot," "Drink It In, Man," "The Gift of Jericho," and "Quiet, Quiet, Quiet." (Don't even get me started on "The List of Jericho" . . . that's for another book!) I even gave myself a challenge to get the word "IT" over. It took a minute, but after repeating it on *Raw* at opportune times over the next few months, I did that too. The critics and fans went from DEMANDING my retirement to proclaiming this run as one of my best ever.

But that "Stupid Idiot" era of Jericho never would've have been so successful had I not committed by planting those seeds early on as the fetid Y2J character. Even though it was hard having people question my skills and relevancy, I committed to the long-term story and endured the criticism, knowing what I was working towards. It's like the story Paul McCartney told about rock critics in 1967 proclaiming the Beatles to be old news because they'd stopped touring and had outlived their welcome, while in reality they were secretly in the studio recording *Sgt. Pepper's Lonely Hearts Club Band*, the greatest album of their career. They ignored the criticism, stayed committed to their art, and had huge success as a result.

So the next time I start a "Rooty Tooty Booty" chant, just shut up and play along, okay?

CHAPTER 12

THE
BRIAN PILLMAN
PRINCIPLE

DO SOMETHING DIFFERENT

I never played by the rules, I never really cared . . .
—SKID ROW, "YOUTH GONE WILD"

Earlier in this palimpsest, you read about the impact that Paul Stanley had on me as a teenager. But as I was growing up and getting involved in the wrestling business, another performer who was just as big of an influence on me was The Heartbreak Kid, Shawn Michaels. I'd go so far as to say that when I started out wrestling, I basically copied him. I grew my hair into a sweet mullet and dyed it canary yellow like Shawn, wore ring gear that was as closely modeled to HBK's as I could afford, and ripped off his trademark high spots move for move. But it didn't take me long to realize that being a direct copy of Shawn, while fine for starters, would put me in a specific box and limit my potential for success.

So by taking a few of Shawn's best qualities, adding some of Paul's magic, and throwing them into a show business blender along with a healthy dollop of me, I now had something. I was never interested in being the "next whomever." I just wanted to be the first Chris Jericho, because I knew if I wanted to make it, I had to do something different.

The late Brian Pillman hammered this principle home to me the one and only time our paths crossed at an ECW show in 1996—his last weekend with the company happened to be my first. We hit it off right away, and I'm guessing that's partly because he knew I had trained in Calgary like he did, and partly because Chris Benoit was a mutual friend.

We sat in the corner of the dressing room/basement of the Lost Battalion Hall in Queens, New York, where Brian filled me in on his upcoming plans to go to WCW and start the new-age Four Horsemen (who would use a "two arms crossed in an X" gesture instead of the iconic "four fingers up" sign) with Benoit and Dean Malenko. He asked me if I would consider being the fourth member and I told him I'd check my busy skedge. Actually, I said, "Absofuckinlutely!" because I would've given up everything and done it in a second. Unfortunately, I never saw Brian again nor heard another word about the new-age Horsemen, so I assume the angle was dropped.

But what I remember most about our conversation was Brian telling me about his decision to reinvent himself as the "Loose Cannon," a subtly crazy hothead who would lash out in uncontrolled outbursts at random. It was a completely different persona from the squeaky-clean babyface he had embodied in the ring for the past decade.

I asked him why he felt the need to change things up, considering the amount of success he'd already had. He looked off into the corner of the room and murmered softly, "If you want to really make it in this business, you have to do something different. Something nobody has ever done before."

Then to illustrate his point, he got up and wandered around the locker room asking people if they had an extra belt to hold up his jeans, because they were the wrong size. Nobody did, so he settled on a piece of rope (like a brown piece of twine that a hobo in a cartoon would wear) that he had "found" beneath one of the tables in the back room. He ran the rope through his belt loops, with bugged-out eyes and a satisfied, crooked grin. Then he walked around the room asking rhetorical questions and making random statements in his raspy voice.

"Have you ever seen the rain?"

"I noticed your shoelaces. Do you like mine?"

"Isn't it great to be living in America?"

Brian didn't say anything over-the-top crazy or offensive, but it was all very weird. And that was the exact image he wanted to portray, because he was doing everything he could to work the WWE and WCW brass into a bidding war. He ended up acting so wacky that he legitimately freaked out some of his peers (Bobby Heenan thought he was totally off his rocker), and even conned Eric Bischoff into giving him his WCW release to fool the fans into thinking the company wanted nothing to do with him. Brian then took that WCW release to Vince McMahon in Stamford, and in one of the biggest double crosses in wrestling history, used it to sign a lucrative WWE multi-year contract.

He built himself from a midsized, midcard, white-meat babyface to a believably dangerous main event heel in the land of the giants. And he did it by doing something that had never been done before.

Sadly, Brian passed away a few years later, so he didn't reach his main event potential, but I never forgot his words. Whether it was a topknot fountain ponytail, different facial hair every week, wearing suits and speaking ten-dollar words in a slow voice, or sportin' a vest with no shirt and a scarf, I always made sure to do something nobody else was doing.

But for me being original just came naturally, and long before I ever met Brian Pillman, I was trying to stand out in any way I could. In the early '90s I painted my nails black, got both ears pierced multiple times, wore eye shadow with a rhinestone choker, put pink streaks in my hair, was one of the first wrestlers to wear kickpads in North America, and even rocked a color-coordinated black-and-white checkerboard suit that made me look like Rick Nielson on the gas. Nothing was too outlandish for me. I never really cared what anybody thought of me, because I knew that no matter their opinion, they would at the very least remember me. I mean, look how much traction I've gotten from wearing that stupid scarf!

I kept the same mindset when I was putting together ideas for my wrestling storylines. With every return to the WWE, I wanted to do something different, which caused my stature within the company to grow with both the fans and the office. As a result, I was allowed more input into my angles.

When AJ Styles debuted at the 2016 Royal Rumble, there was a huge buzz about him throughout the entire WWE Universe. Everybody was excited to see what he could do within the company . . . except the boss himself. Vince never gets too excited at first by new hires who have made their names elsewhere. Just like when I initially arrived in the WWE, all of the fanfare generated from AJ's debut didn't mean that much to Mr. McMahon. As with every performer who ever drew a WWE paycheck, until you stepped into one of Vince's rings, nothing else you had accomplished during your career really mattered. The fans might have been thrilled to see what AJ could bring to the table, but Vince would believe it when he saw it with his own two eyes. That's why I was excited to work with The Phenomenal One and help make his entrance into my company as smooth as possible.

I had the perfect opportunity the night after the Rumble, when I showed up in Miami for *Raw* and found out that AJ and I were working together for the first time ever. But when I heard that the match was only meant to be a one-night thing, I went to Vince and suggested that AJ and I start an angle that would culminate at the next PPV a few weeks later. He agreed, and after that PPV Vince was so impressed with our chemistry that he decided to stretch the storyline out all the way to WrestleMania.

Over the next few months, we constructed an exciting narrative filled with countless twists and turns along the way. AJ and I started as rivals, then eventually shook hands and decided to work together as a unit. But since this was the WWE, I knew that it would be hard to convince the fans that one of us wasn't going to turn on the other . . . which was the exact plan. So when we beat The New Day in a nontitle match on *Raw* leading to a rematch for the WWE tag titles the following week in Chicago, I knew we needed to come up with something that would convince fans that AJ and I were going to be around for the long haul.

So I had the idea of producing an AJ-Jericho team T-shirt that would go on sale exclusively at the arena in Chicago, leading the fans in attendance to think, *Well, they have their own merch, so they must be sticking around for a while.* I called the WWE merchandise team to find out the chances of producing Y2AJ T-shirts on short notice. (Cool Author's aside: I know Y2AJ is a pretty brutal name and that's why I wanted it used. Considering we were designed to be a short-term team, there was no reason to think of something better, but if we ever team again I promise we'll think of a catchier moniker.)

I knew that doing a one-off shirt was possible because we'd made one for the Y2J twenty-fifth anniversary show a few months earlier, so I was surprised when the merch guys said they didn't know if there was enough time to produce them. That didn't fly for me, as I knew they could make it happen if they really had to, so in the fine tradition of Principle #5, I politely explained how important it was to have them ready. I hung up the phone and promptly called Vince, who liked the idea so much that he wanted them ready to sell online on WWE.com the next day, as well as in the arena the following week.

Armed with that info, I called the merch guys back and asked again if they could have them ready on time. When the dude told me they thought they could do it, I said, "Great, I'll let Vince know! Oh and by the way, he wants them up on dot-com tomorrow."

Needless to say, the shirts were ready to go the next day, and while they didn't sell all that well, the desired effect was achieved. By merely seeing that the merch was available, the fans assumed that Y2AJ was a real team who was about to have a substantial run, not a couple of guys who were going to break up as quickly as they got together.

I ended up turning on Styles in Chicago after a great match, and the heat was nuclear. Fans were genuinely pissed off that I had attacked my new partner, especially after such an excellent performance, thereby spoiling the potential of a Styles-Jericho team and all the classics we could've had in the future. But the angriest of them all was the contingent of fans who'd been suckered into happily buying a T-shirt for a team that was together for less than a week.

First of all, to those of you that did buy the Y2AJ shirt, I'm sorry you fell for it . . . but you have to admit that it was something diabolically different that helped get our angle over and added a shitload of intrigue to what we were about to do at WrestleMania, right?

Secondly, if you still have the shirt, stop bitching and put it up for sale on eBay! After all, it's a limited edition rarity and probably worth a lot more than the twenty-five bucks you paid for it.

See . . . my turning heel could actually make you money!

CHAPTER 13

THE AMERICA'S FUNNIEST HOME VIDEOS PRINCIPLE

LET IT GO

Don't be afraid to lose
what was never meant to be . . .
—NELSON, "AFTER THE RAIN"

A toddler swings a plastic baseball bat into his unsuspecting father's plums.

An overweight auntie breaks a chair when she sits down at the family cookout.

A dog and cat play catch with a bocce ball.

All of these scenarios are hilariously cheesy or cheesily hilarious, depending on what side of the entertainment coin you're on—and all of them are trademarks of one of the longest-running American television institutions in the world today.

I'm talking about *America's Funniest Home Videos*.

Whether you've seen original host Bob Saget troll the audience with his brutal puns and nerdy demeanor or his successor Tom Bergeron's more subdued, smooth charm and dry, subtle humor, we've all watched a least one episode.

As a matter of fact, I used to watch *AFV* all the time. I just never thought I'd almost end up hosting the damn thing.

But that's what happened when Bergeron announced he was leaving the show after fifteen seasons in 2015 and through a set of strange extenuating circumstances, I was courted by show creator, Vin Di Bona, to be the new face of the franchise. At first I wasn't sure about it, but I quickly realized that I had what it took to be the new kid on the block (and I ain't talkin' about Jordan Knight).

It was a massive opportunity, as being the host of the iconic *AFV* would give me a chance to sit at the top of the syndicated television totem pole. But I'm getting ahead of myself, so in the words of the mighty Kick Axe (shout out to Kerns and Fitz), let's go "back to the beginning."

After so many flirtations with mainstream prime-time gigs, from competing on *Dancing with the Stars*, to hosting the ABC game show *Downfall*, the SyFy Channel competition show *Robot Combat League*, and the Fuse TV singing show *Redemption Song*, I felt it was only a matter of time before something big came up and helped me break fully into the Hollywood big leagues.

When I was approached by Di Bona's reps about the possibility of hosting *AFV*, I was kind of surprised. A few months prior, I had met with an executive at Disney named Dan Cohen whose wife was a big wig at *AFV*, which I assumed was the connection here. It reminded me that there was never a meeting too small to take in Hollywood, because you never knew who you might meet or how it might pay off.

I had my initial meeting with Vin and a few of his producers at a popular restaurant in West Hollywood. Since I'd been given word by my Disney contact that Vin was looking for a younger, more contemporary host than the previous one, I decided to forgo the typical sports coat/suit uniform of the average Hollywood wannabe and went with a classic Jericho scarf-vest combo that was more David Lee Roth than Gene Rayburn. My plan worked, as Vin and I had a fun, easy-flowing conversation about, the show, '50s crooners, and '60s singer-songwriters who played guitar and sang at the same time, *Battle of the Network Stars* (a '70s celebrity sports competition show that I loved when I was a kid), and classic cars (I faked my way through a debate as to whether a 1967 SS 427 Camaro was better than a 1970 Z28 quite admirably, if I do say so myself).

A few hours later, I got a call from Dan saying that on behalf of the group and himself, I had passed the audition . . . at least the first round of it. Vin was convinced I had the charm to take over the reins of his twenty-five-year-old franchise and was interested in organizing a follow-up meeting. Even though it was made very clear to me that Vin was also talking to other people about hosting the show, it was nice to know that I was on the short list of Di Bona. (I couldn't resist!)

Over the next few months, I attended further lunches, sat in on a panel discussion on the future of social media held by Berkeley University (Vin was on their board of directors), had countless *AFV*-related phone calls, and even invited Vin to SummerSlam to watch my match against Bray Wyatt. After all that, I was really starting to believe that I might be the chosen one.

With each meeting, it became clearer to me that I could do this gig better than anybody else and all of my years of show business training had led me to the brink of landing the job of a lifetime. I felt that nobody else could match my combination of experience, improv ability, on-camera comfort-ability, worldwide fan base, and rugged good looks that were important to distinguish Chris Jericho from both previous *AFV* hosts and its almost outdated image.

In the meantime, my agent, Barry Bloom, and my lawyers negotiated with ABC and Vin's lawyers on the finer points of the deal (how much they were willing to pay me per episode). When the dust settled, a deal was agreed upon—but not yet signed— that would see me making close to seven figures for just three weeks of work per season. I couldn't have been happier and I was ready for my close-up, Mr. Di Bona.

I was starting to settle into the notion that the gig was actually going to be mine, when I began hearing some odd comments from one of the *AFV* execs. In a way, he kind of let it slip that ABC had already chosen their preferred host, and that host wasn't me.

Around this time, I started hearing rumors about who that network-approved host might be. There were two names in particular that kept popping up, both of whom were familiar to me because I'd worked with them in the past. The first was Mario Lopez, who had rubbed me the wrong way whenever we met for years, culminating with a war of wills during a punishing round of Twister Hoopla on *The Ellen DeGeneres Show* (read the whole story in my classic parable, *The Best in the World: At What I Have No Idea*). The second was Alfonso Ribeiro, with whom I'd clashed on my ill-fated stint on the awful Fox singing show *Celebrity Duets* ten years prior (drink in that whole story in my award-winning, modern-day morality play, *Undisputed*). Knowing I was up against those muttonheads made me want to throw up in my mouth a little. If I didn't get the gig, I didn't get the gig, but please not to one of those guys!

Then I was summoned to LA to host an actual episode of the show in front of a live audience, and I knew that this was the chance I was waiting for to show what I could really do. This wasn't me standing in for a scene or two either; this was a fully produced, airable episode that was to take place right after a Tom Bergeron–hosted taping.

But in a "when it rains sharks, it pours" moment, I'd also been cast as Bruce the Ride Attendant in *Sharknado 3*, the third installment of the immensely popular SyFy Channel C-grade horror series. It was a good role, and I knew there would be huge press behind it due to the buzz the previous two films had garnered. The only drawback was that I was supposed to film my scenes on the same day I was required for rehearsals for the *AFV* screen test. With shrewd planning by Barry Bloom and some luck in making my flights, I finished my two days on set at Universal Studios in Orlando at 2 p.m. and then headed straight to the airport to catch a 4 p.m. plane to LAX to make my 9 p.m. rehearsal. But it was worth making *Sharknado* happen, as it was a tremendous experience and I got to work with some great people, including leading man Ian Ziering, who advised me how to get eaten by a CGI shark (flail as much as possible so the computer programmers had to make the shark's movements more grandiose), and my childhood crush Kim Richards (*Escape from Witch Mountain* like a maafuckaa)!

I landed at LAX at 8:30 p.m. and went straight to the studio. Vin was waiting for me and meticulously led me through the camera blocking for the segments I'd be hosting, and explained what would be expected of me the following evening. He also gave me an acoustic guitar and suggested I sing a song during the tapings, as he wanted me to stand out in any way possible and thought if I came up with a pretty little ditty to sing for the audience, it might be fun. I hadn't played guitar and sung at the same time since high school, and I wasn't a James Hetfield–level musician who could do that easily, but in the fine Hollywood tradition of never saying no to anything, I told him it was a great idea and that I was going to change my stage name to Elvis Jericho when I was done.

I remember reading when Sting (and I ain't talking about the guy in the makeup) was first learning to play and sing at the same time, he wrote songs with space in between the chords so he could concentrate solely on his vocals (e.g., "Walking on the Moon"). In that spirit, I worked up a tune using hanging power chords and a staccato rhythm change that enabled me to play while I sang my brilliant lyrics, which went something like this:

Now it is time for *America's Funniest Videos,*
Fun for your friends, and your parents and your kiddios,
So watch with me now and in laughter we will join,
As we watch little kids hit their dads in the groin . . .

Not exactly Dylan's "Tangled Up in Blue," but it fit the vibe of
the show and worked perfectly for what I was trying to accomplish. Vin got a laugh out of it as well and made no bones about
the fact that I was his front runner for the job.

"I want you to get this gig," he said to me in a matter-of-fact
tone. His words gave me confidence, but in the back of my mind
a worm of doubt was burrowing, because I wondered, *What does
he mean by "want"?* If he's the boss and he wants me to get the
gig, why doesn't he just give it to me? At that point, it was clear
that he wasn't the only one making the final decisions and I still
had some convincing to do for the hold-outs in the Lopez Ribeiro
camps.

Then he asked if I minded covering the Fozzy "F" tattoo on my
left hand, because he didn't want "to give anybody an excuse
not to hire you as the host." Apparently, there were some evil
overlords who were looking for any reason not to choose me . . .
but it was now my mission to erase their inhibitions.

The next night, I paced the floor of my dressing room before
the big show, wearing a John Varvatos suit (no tie; too stuffy for
the image I wanted to portray) and practicing my song. A parade
of well-wishers came in to give me last-minute thumbs-ups and
words of encouragement, including Tom Bergeron himself who
I knew from my time on *Dancing with the Stars.*

"Just be yourself and have fun!" he advised.

That's exactly what I did.

After Tom's taping was finished, I stood in the wings as the announcer explained to the audience that there was one more episode to be filmed that day, featuring a guest host . . . Chris Jericho!

My appearance had been kept under wraps the whole night,
so it was a surprise to the crowd when my name was announced.

Thankfully, there was a coterie of Jerichoholics in attendance who gave me a great reception that quickly spread around the studio when people figured out I was "somebody" and they didn't want to be left out of the fun.

Throughout the next hour, I ran that damn show like I was Johnny Carson in 1975: I kept people entertained, made them laugh when it was required, and quieted them down when it was time to watch the videos.

My Elvis Jericho pretty little ditty (and I ain't talkin' about the Red Hot Chili Peppers) went over big, especially when I used my Fozzy front man skills to lead the crowd in a clapping sing-along. Vin had encouraged me to break the invisible wall between the host and the audience, so I prowled the stage telling jokes, giving fans high fives, and even sitting on a hefty African American lady who was screaming and clapping for me like I was Hercules from *The Nutty Professor*.

"You're my favorite host, Jericho! I hope you get the job!" she repeated excitedly while her husband took pictures of us on his iPhone. I was a hit with those two and most of the rest of the audience as well, and I felt like I'd nailed it. I've always been overcritical of everything I do (I still don't care for my 1999 *Raw* debut promo with The Rock), but at that time, on that night, I knew I'd killed it and wouldn't have changed a thing.

My prospective boss apparently felt the same way, as he grabbed me in a bear hug when I walked off stage with the cheers of the crowd still ringing in the studio.

"Excellent, Chris! You made me proud!"

I hugged him back and thanked him for the opportunity, then walked back to my dressing room to process what had just happened. Barry joined me a few minutes later, and we jumped up and down in celebration like a couple of *Star Wars* nerds who had just found an advance copy of Episode VIII.

It was one of the best nights of my professional career . . . for about another seven minutes.

Barry and I were in the midst of our Dagobah dance when one of the *AFV* higher-ups (not Vin) barged in, babbling so rapidly and incoherently that I can only assume he was coked up.

"You did a good job, Chris, but ABC has already made their decision and the guy they chose just blew them away from the start so it's too bad but they thought he was just so great, and it's pretty much a done deal but thanks for coming out and . . ."

The person continuing speed-rambling as I mouthed to Barry, "What the hell are they talking about?"

The Yeyo Kid finished the tirade and bounced out the door, but at that point my buzz had been killed, brought back to life by Melisandre, and then killed again. I should've felt triumphant, but after that asshole's rambling, I just wanted to go to bed.

The next day, I shrugged off the previous night's bad vibes and went to a recording studio to track voice-overs for my episode. They took a little more time than I would've liked, as Vin was watching over my shoulder having me repeat the lines until he got the exact take he was looking for, right down to each syllable. He reminded me a lot of Vince because he knew precisely what he wanted, and he wasn't going to be satisfied until he got it. I eventually gave him what he was looking for and the first of what hopefully would be many episodes of *AFV* hosted by Chris Jericho was complete.

When I left the studio, I didn't know if I had gotten the gig, but I knew I had done all I could and there was nothing left to do but wait . . . .and wait . . . and wait. Over the next two months, the only word I received was that I was indeed a finalist for the job—along with Ribeiro Lopez.

Finally, eight weeks later, the phone rang and I saw the name VIN DI BONA on my screen. I ran up the stairs into my office and answered nervously.

"Hey, Vin, how are you?"

"I'm good, Chris."

Fuck. I knew by his tone that I hadn't gotten the gig.

"I just wanted to call you myself to tell you . . . that we've decided to go with somebody else as the new host of *AFV*."

Ugh. I knew it. I felt like I'd been kicked in the ballbag by Braun Strowman.

Now, I don't take no for an answer in most cases, but I also know when the time comes to accept defeat and step back. I knew the *AFV* train had left the station, and there was nothing I could do to change Vin's decision. I could beg him for a second chance or demand to know the reason why I didn't get chosen, but I knew it was better to just take it like a man and get off the phone. Besides, it was pointless to ask him what I could've done differently or who got the job instead of me, because it really didn't matter.

However, before I could hang up with my dignity intact, Vin continued with a few more details.

"We've decided to go with somebody with a little more comedic experience, someone who can handle the voice-overs (Angry Author's note: Fuck those fuckin' voice-overs) a little differently than you did. You really did a great job and I think there are going to be some opportunities for us to work together again in the future. I'll be in touch in about a month."

"Okay, Vin, thanks again for the opportunity and hopefully we can talk soon."

I hung up the phone and saw that the time of the call was 1 minute and 48 seconds. Fourteen months of schmoozing, phone calls, meetings, and auditions had been boiled down to a 108-second rejection notice. I was pissed off because I truly felt that *AFV* had been MY gig to lose . . . and I'd lost it.

I went downstairs and poured myself a Yeah Boy and didn't stop at one. I was filled with a dozen different emotions, including self-doubt, loss, and frustration. That phone call had shaken me more than anything else in my forty-three years of existence.

My professional depression (cool song title) deepened a few weeks later, when I was at a Rush concert in Houston and got the news that Alfonso Ribeiro had officially gotten the job. I read his statement online (while Geddy Lee laid down the bass line in "Roll the Bones") where he promised to bring new energy to the show and to even perform the Carlton dance from time to time. Seriously? That's the last thing I needed to hear. I hated that fuckin' thing when he did it twenty years ago on *The Fresh Prince of Bel-Air,* and it hadn't gotten any better since.

After the Ribeiro announcement, I was barraged by a mix of emotions, including jealousy, anger, and revenge (thoughts of calling Speewee to plant a bag of cocaine in Alfonso's car ran briefly through my mind). But once the news came out, it felt better to have closure, and at least I could take solace in the fact that I had beaten Mario Lopez. (Technically, I suppose he could've been the first runner-up, but in my mind I had blown him away and it's my book, so deal with it.)

More importantly, I started to let the poison sting of rejection fade away. There was no reason to continue to second-guess myself, because I knew I had done everything within my ability to get the gig. I gave the best performance I could have and the rest was out of my hands. It was time to let it go.

To help me get over the rejection, I asked the advice of some of my veteran show biz friends including William Shatner who said, "If I dwelled upon every gig I didn't get, I would've quit show biz after a year." He was in his seventh decade of show biz, so I figured he knew what he was talking about and took his words to heart.

My *Sharknado* simpatico, Ian Ziering, told me a similar story about how he lost *The Price Is Right* hosting gig to Drew Carey a few years earlier.

"You can't let it bring you down, man. It wasn't meant to be, which means there's another gig out there for you that is."

My friends were right. I decided to let *AFV* go for good, and subsequently it became just another gig in a sea of gigs I didn't get. But somewhere in a dusty warehouse in New Mexico, lying on a shelf beside the Ark of the Covenant, there's a locked wooden box with a tape inside of an episode of *America's Funniest Home Videos* hosted by Chris Jericho . . .

EPILOGUE

While I was writing this very chapter, after not hearing from Vin for sixteen months, I got a call from his office asking about possibly doing another project together.

To be continued . . .

CHAPTER 14

THE
MIKE
LOZANSKI
PRINCIPLE

STAND UP FOR WHAT
YOU BELIEVE IN

Get up stand up, stand up for your rights . . .
—BOB MARLEY, "GET UP, STAND UP"

A few months before I moved from Winnipeg to Calgary to train with the Hart brothers, I was hanging out at the local strip club down the street from my house called the Ville. The place was as classy as it sounds, darkly lit with fake-wood-paneled walls that reeked of stale smoke and cheap beer. However, due to the wonders of fake IDs, my friends and I had been hanging out there since we were fifteen years old. So even though it was a shithole, it was our shithole.

That night, a DJ who resembled Bob Ross was playing the hot tunes of the fall of '89, including healthy doses of Guns N'

Roses, Roxette, Alannah Myles, and the Northern Pikes (there's some Canadiana for you) while walking the floor with a cordless mic asking the scattered patrons random questions in between dances. He stuck the mic in the face of a guy who looked exactly like Barney Gumble and asked, "My man! What do you want Shelley Sensation to do tonight?"

"Take your clothes off!!" Barney screamed at the top of his lungs to nobody in particular. Considering we were in a peeler joint, it was a fair request.

It just so happened that I'd been staring at said Shelley Sensation from the moment she got onstage, and she'd looked back at me a few times with a beguiling smile. Now, keep in mind that Canadian strip clubs are different than American ones, as instead of hanging around all night hustling for dances, the stripper does four onstage shows a day, consisting of four songs each. When her show is over, she leaves the premises until the next show, which is usually two or three hours later.

That meant that if I didn't approach Shelley as soon as she left the stage, I wouldn't see her again for hours. So I power walked over as she slid a silk robe onto her amazingly toned, naked body and chatted her up. She seemed engaged enough, so it didn't seem out of line to ask her for her number (I mean she obviously wasn't there to make money, but to hook up with goofy-ass teenagers, right?), but my bubble was burst when she said, "I'd give you my number but my boyfriend probably wouldn't like that. He's a pro wrestler too."

She said "pro wrestler too," because I had told her I WAS a professional wrestler, not that I was GOING to wrestling school in a few months. But that's nitpicking, isn't it? Besides. I wanted to know who this fancy pants wrestler "boyfriend" was, so I asked her his name.

"I'm dating Mike Lozanski," she said with a smile.

Well, that changed everything.

I knew who Mike Lozanski was because I'd seen him on TV, wrestling for the local Winnipeg promotion run by Tony

Condello. Not only was he a good-looking guy and a pretty good wrestler . . . but he was banging this gorgeous stripper, too? I decided right then I wouldn't mind meeting this Lozanski cat and learning a thing or two from him.

I ended up meeting him a few months later after I finished wrestling school, through Brett Como, a talented performer who had also been on Condello's TV. I hit it off with both of them instantly and they took me under their wings right from the start.

Brett was a sarcastic rocker dude like me, but Mike was a charismatic schmoozer who made friends with almost everybody he met. He had big-league confidence with the touch of arrogance needed to get out of the local Calgary scene and make it to the next level. And that's what he did.

With only a few years in the business under his belt, Mike had already wrestled in New Zealand, Japan, Mexico, all across Canada, and over a dozen states. He also came from a wealthy family, which meant he didn't have to worry about how much he was getting paid or what expenses he might incur along the way. That was the perfect situation for Como and me, because Mike paid for all of our gas and our food bills whenever we traveled together. The drawback to that was it meant Mike called the shots. If he wanted to drive all night or stop for food or head to the ghetto looking for weed (as described in my true-crime novel, *A Lion's Tale*), Como and I would have to follow. But it wasn't such a bad deal because we got to drive across the country and work in places like northern British Columbia and southern California, which most of the other guys in Calgary didn't have the chance to. I felt bad about that at times and even asked Mike if my tag-team partner, Lance Storm, could join us for a thirty-six-hour drive to a show in Pomona, California.

"Listen, Chris, you're not going to be a tag team forever, so you need to take the bookings you can get and not worry about your partner."

I felt bad relaying that to Lance, even though he understood and had no problem with it. It was Mike's decision and I had to go along with it, just as it was Mike's decision for us to drive across the continent to work a television taping in Wichita, Kansas.

When we arrived in Wichita, we found out that the promoter Christopher Love wasn't all that he claimed to be. In fact, he was full of shit. He had surrounded himself with a ragtag collection of yes-men and cronies who boasted about how big they were in the business, even though I hadn't heard of a single one of them. I had a bad vibe about the place to begin with, which got worse when Love decided at the last second that he didn't want to use Como. He claimed it was because Brett was too small, even though he'd seen pictures of all three of us and knew exactly what he was getting when he agreed to bring us in.

Mike was furious. Love had made him look bad because he had gotten the three of us booked, and after the marathon journey we'd gone through to get there, he wasn't able to deliver the opportunity he'd promised. Brett told him pretty much right away that he didn't give a shit and had no problem with the two of us still doing the show, but Mike wasn't having it.

"No fucking way! Love promised to use the three of us, so either we all work or none of us do."

I did a mental double take at Mike's words, because I had made that long drive and dealt with all the bullshit to get to Wichita as well, so I wasn't as keen on just turning around and going home without taking advantage of the opportunity. I mean, what if I had a good match that ended up on TV and got me more bookings in America? Working in the States was a rare thing for me at that time, and I didn't want to let this chance slip away. If it had been up to me I would've worked the show and given Como half my payoff, but to Mike this wasn't about the money; it was about standing up for what he believed in. He'd been lied to, which to him was unacceptable, so now we were going to stick together. I eventually saw his point and backed him when he told Love he was going to have to use all three of us, or none of us at all.

"Fine, then the three of you can fuck off back to Canada. I don't really give a shit," the fat bastard snarled.

So we fucked off back to Canada empty handed and matchless. But we left Kansas with our heads held high and smiles on our faces, because we had stuck together and stood up for what we felt was right. And that was a damn good feeling.

Unfortunately, Mike and I grew apart over the years, and even though he had some success working as Mike Anthony in Memphis, ECW, and WCW, we didn't really cross paths too often before he passed away at just thirty-five years old in 2003. I felt awful when I found out about his death, because I should've reached out to him and been a better friend during the problematic latter stages of his life. But I still think about him often, because he was a big influence in the early days of my career, and I might not have made it as far as I did without him, his friendship, and the lesson he taught me in Wichita back in 1991.

Thanks, Mikey.

MIKE'S CONCEPT of standing up for what you believe in has come up time and time again in my WWE career, but most recently in 2016 when I was working with AJ Styles. As we discussed earlier in this fine compendium, I was really excited to wrestle AJ when he first signed with the company.

He was a tremendous performer with a dazzling array of offense, but I found it odd that whenever he won a match, it was always with the top-rope Phenomenal Forearm or the Calf Crusher submission, despite the fact that his Styles Clash finish was already really popular and synonymous with him.

Whenever he teased the Styles Clash, people went bananas (Pat Patterson™) with anticipation only to be let down when the move was thwarted, so when I suggested we use the Clash as the actual finish to one of our matches, I was told that it had been unofficially banned by Vince. Someone had brought it to his attention that a few guys had supposedly been hurt by the move, even though it was one of the easiest bumps I would ever take in my career (Mr. Socko was the easiest by far). Here's how it worked. AJ would pick up his opponent like he was going to give him a piledriver, but instead of sitting down he would simply fall forward and faceplant the guy. So you would land mostly on your chest and knees, but the illusion would be that your face had been smashed into the mat. It was a piece of piss to take and a great move, so I decided I would make it my mission to get it unbanned.

When we worked our third match at the Fast Break PPV, I thought it was the perfect opportunity to bust it out in the WWE for the first time and show Vince that it wasn't as dangerous as he had heard. If it was safe enough for one of his top guys to take, then it must be okay for everybody else, right?

Since this was one of AJ's established finishes, I didn't want to just take it and kick out with no merit, so we came up with an idea where he'd hit me with it and I'd barely kick out, only to have him roll me right into the Calf Crusher for the tap-out victory. In the fine tradition of a principle that didn't make the book, "It's easier to ask for forgiveness than permission," I figured if Vince really didn't want us to use the move, we would hear about it after. Thankfully, he didn't say anything because it was a safe-looking "Whattamanouver!" that got a massive reaction from the crowd. It also got a massive NEGATIVE reaction from the Internet smart mark contingent, who accused me of taking the Styles Clash, just so I could kick out of it and continue AJ's "WWE burial." (You should've heard how outraged they were when I actually pinned him at WrestleMania . . . apparently, it was the worst decision since Hillary deleted her emails.)

In reality, my strategy wasn't to kick out of the Clash to bury AJ, but to take the move on camera so that Vince could see with his own two eyes (and I ain't talkin' about Fairies Wear Boots) just how safe it was. Step one of my plan worked because we didn't get any flak, and it was treated as just another great false finish in a match full of them.

The second step of the plan was to use it again as a near fall in front of over a hundred thousand fans at WrestleMania 32 in Dallas. Once again, we built the match to the perfect point so when AJ hit the Clash, the crowd exploded. They were sure it was the finish, until I kicked out at 2.9999 seconds, leading to another huge pop, this one of disappointment. It worked perfectly, and my mission of clearing the good name of the Styles Clash was almost complete.

The perfect chance to finish what I started (and I ain't talkin' about Eddie Van Halen) presented itself the next night when the main event of *Raw* was a fatal fourway between me, AJ, Cesaro, and Kevin Owens to decide the number one contender for the WWE Championship. The finish was AJ over me and that's when I knew the time was right to strike.

I went into Vince's office to pitch the finish, but there was one very important rule I had to remember: I could not use the name STYLES CLASH at any time. I had a hunch that while Vince might be against the theoretical move called the Styles Clash, he also might not know what it actually was. But since he had already seen the move, as I had taken it twice already, that would mean he would know what I was talking about if I described it without actually calling it by name.

"Vince, do you remember the move we used at Mania yesterday where AJ picked me up like a piledriver, but just fell forward and pancaked my face instead?"

"Of course. It got a great reaction."

"Yes it did. That's why I think we should use it as the finish tonight. It's easy, it's over, and it could add another weapon to AJ's arsenal."

"I love it, let's do it."

There you have it. AJ pinned me with it later that night and biggity-bam, the Styles Clash was officially back in business, thanks to yours truly. So, Constant Reader, whenever you see him use it (including giving it to Roman Reigns on the floor a few months later), holla atcha boy, Jericho.

And to all the Internet smarks who threw so much shade at me the first time I kicked out of it, I accept your apology and hope you've learned your lesson, you stupid idiots.

ON NOVEMBER 13, 2015, there was a brutal attack in Paris where ISIS terrorists initiated multiple bombings and shootings, killing 130 people in total, with 89 of them being at an Eagles of Death Metal concert inside a venue called the Bataclan. That attack caused great unrest among European rock fans, and I know this because I was there . . . Fozzy had played a gig the same night in Rotterdam, Netherlands, only 285 miles away from Paris. Even more chilling was the fact that we had a Paris gig of our own scheduled for exactly one week later.

The entire country was in mass chaos and it was a difficult time to be touring in Europe. As a band, we were in a difficult position. On one hand, all of our families wanted us to come home, and the fact that a slew of big bands had already cancelled their European shows didn't strengthen our case. Within days, U2, Motörhead, Lamb of God, and Papa Roach all postponed their tours and got the hell out of Dodge. And while we considered doing the same, Rich and I eventually decided we didn't want to do that to our fans. In this difficult time, people needed something to take their minds off the tragedy, so what would it help to cancel our shows and give the terrorists another small win over the world? In the end, we made a unanimous decision as a band to stand up for what we believed in and continue the tour.

The following week wasn't easy. There was an eerie feeling at every show leading up to Paris, and attendance was understandably way down, as the last thing a lot of people wanted to do was go to a rock show. It all came to a head that Friday when we showed up for our concert at Le Forum in Vauréal, a suburb of Paris. I was a little freaked out playing in France only seven days after the tragedy, but I let go of those thoughts quickly the moment I hit the stage.

We had a band discussion before the gig and decided it didn't matter how many people showed up; they were going to get one hell of a rock show. Fozzy's motto of "ten or ten thousand" never meant as much to us as it did that night. We had a job to entertain the fans and help them forget this tragedy, and we were going to do that to the best of our abilities, no matter who came.

When our set began, I was pleasantly surprised to see a couple hundred fans in the room and happy to hear they were a loud crowd right from the start. These Fozzy fanatics were truly hardcore, ready for a good time, and so were we. The show went by smoothly, with the highlight being the "minute of noise" we requested for the fallen Parisians. Let me just say that those two hundred people sounded like twenty thousand, as they roared as loud as they could for sixty seconds. It was such an emotional moment and was as deep a connection to an audience as I've ever felt.

What made the night even more special was how many of our fans thanked us for playing the show. They were genuinely appreciative of the fact that we had shown the balls to not cancel, even in the face of potential danger. It reminded me of when I toured Iraq with the WWE three years running to visit the US military, and spent the entire time having soldiers of all ages tell me how much it meant to them that the WWE had come to see them. *They* were the ones who were living through the horrors of war, but *we* were the ones being treated like heroes. That night at Le Forum gave me the same feeling, especially after our encounter with Lionel, who was working at Le Forum as our backstage assistant for the day. His job was to stock the dressing room with food, hook up our wifi, bring us towels or ice, and basically take care of anything we needed.

He was a fun guy who spoke fairly good English and we had some brief conversations, but it wasn't until after the show that I learned he'd been trapped in the Bataclan seven days earlier.

Lionel was watching the Eagles of Death Metal show when the shooting started, and ended up barricading himself with a group of others in an upstairs room by pushing a refrigerator against the door. He and twelve other potential victims waited in total silence for the next three hours as the gunshots cracked outside the door. He even had to lean into the fridge to hold it in place at one point, as the terrorists tried to force their way into the room. Eventually, the attackers moved on, choosing to continue the massacre elsewhere.

But what surprised me the most was after that horrible experience, Lionel was back at another concert just one week later. I didn't understand how he could do that.

"I have to . . . this is my job and I love music," he said with a heavy accent. "And if I don't come to work tonight I miss out on seeing Fozzy. The terrorists would then take something else from me, and I wasn't going to let that happen."

I praised him for standing up for what he believed it, and he reciprocated.

"It means everything to your fans in Paris that you played tonight, even for the ones who didn't come. Thank you for making us happy in this terrible time."

All I can say is,"*Merci d'être la Lionel! C'est un honneur de jouer pour vous et les gens merveilleux de Paris.*"

Google it.

(Thanks to Kevin Owens for the translation!)

CHAPTER 15

THE
TED
IRVINE
PRINCIPLE

YOU GOTTA
SELL YOURSELF

Hunger, I want it so bad I can taste it.
It drives me mad to see it wasted . . .
—KICK AXE, "HUNGER"

When I first started thinking about getting into the wrestling business, my dad gave me a piece of crucial advice: "You have to sell yourself. When you're starting out, nobody is going to pick up the phone and call you. You have to be the one to call them."

I can affirm all these years later that he was absolutely right. You gotta sell yourself, maaan!

I'm not sure if this was his mindset when he was breaking into the NHL, or just what he came to believe after his pro hockey career was over, but the bottom line (because Stone Ted said so) was that his message was driven into my head early in my career, and I've heeded that advice ever since.

That's why after only a few months in the business (despite my obvious inexperience), I started making highlight videos of my matches using the best high spots I could cull from grainy, jumpy VHS recordings. Then I wrote up a resume listing the meager three companies I'd worked for, along with my college degree info. For a reference, I included the name of the manager at the IGA grocery store where I had worked my last real job, as I'm sure my skills as a meat slicer were just what Vince McMahon was looking for. (Maybe I was hoping to get that coveted Donny Deli gimmick?)

I sent that tape and resume to every promoter I had an address for, including guys in New Zealand, Australia, and Greenland . . . some of whom (unbeknownst to me) hadn't run shows since the '70s. Even when I received no reply (and I ain't talkin' about the Beatles), or got the packages sent back RETURN TO SENDER (and I ain't talkin' about Elvis), at least I was trying to get something rolling and not just sitting on my ass waiting for the phone to ring.

I wasn't ignored completely, as I did get a letter back from the Texas-based Global Wrestling Federation. When I ecstatically opened the envelope, I found what was basically a wrestling version of a "Dear John" letter from booker Bill Eadie. But there was a silver lining, because even though he wasn't interested in bringing me in, he was very complimentary of my tape and told me I had potential (I've still never met Mr. Eadie, but I'd like to thank him for taking the time to write that letter). His words were as powerful to me as "Klaatu, Verata, Necto" were to Ash Williams, because they gave me a modicum of confidence that my plan to get booked *could* work. I had taken a chance and put myself out there and had moved a step forward in return.

But I know from experience that it's not always easy to sell yourself. It takes a lot of chutzpah to pick up the phone and tell somebody how valuable you are to their business or project, but it has to be done—even if they don't respond. You have to keep hammering on that door no matter how exhausting or embarrassing it may be.

You could change the lesson in this chapter to "Stay Determined" or "If You Want Something Done, Do It Yourself," because both of those are basically saying the same thing. If you believe your plan is right, then stick with it. That's an ideal that I use on a micro level as well as a macro level. I employ it all the time to get my ideas across when putting together a match or writing a song. Once I get what I believe is a good idea in my head, I have no problem pushing it on whomever the hapless soul is who attempts to oppose me.

Just ask The Big Show.

Back in 2009, we were the best tag team in the business (the WWE called us "Jerishow," but I didn't like the name and never used it on TV once), and on certain nights when I referred to myself as the "Best in the World" I really meant it. I had a great sense of who my character was and how I wanted my matches to go, and even though in theory being part of a successful tag team means you should compromise, I didn't really do that. Whenever Show had an invariably inferior idea, I would listen, nod my head, and calmly praise him. Then I would explain why my idea was better and wouldn't take no for answer (see chapter 5) until he agreed to do it my way. He always agreed, usually by throwing up his hands and stomping out of the room, mumbling, "Fine, I'm just a big stupid giant . . . what do I know?"

He still has no problem reminding me how my pit-bull tenacity mentally exhausted him until he finally had to tap out and agree to do it my way. That was a smart move, because my way usually was the right way.

That's half the battle when it comes to selling yourself . . . you have to commit (chapter 11) to whatever you are selling. People have to believe that what you are proposing is a must-see no-brainer and they can't live their lives without it or you.

I once read that when John Travolta was still doing auditions, he went into the room with the mindset that he had gotten the part already. He just had to convince the casting directors that he was the only man for the job and hiring anybody else was a foolhardy (Matt and Jeff's slow cousin) decision.

I'm sure it's a lot easier for John Travolta in 2017 to think that way than it was for 1976 John Travolta, while walking into Brian De Palma's office to read for the part of Billy Nolan in *Carrie*. But like young John, I believe you gotta have that confidence, no matter how early on you may be in your career, because you can't afford not to sell yourself at all times.

As of this writing, I'm in my seventeenth year in the WWE and even after all that time, I still discuss every segment I'm in with Vince, because if I don't and something goes awry, I'll get in trouble.

Case in point. In 2013 I did a *Highlight Reel* with The Miz, Wade Barrett, and Brad Maddox that was a shipwreck from the get-go. It was poorly written, filled with bad comedy that got no reaction from the live audience, and a weird clip from Barrett's new movie awkwardly sandwiched in the middle for no apparent reason. There was zero chemistry between the four of us, Maddox forgot his lines, and I made it worse with some bad improv. The whole thing came across forced and ended flat, and the only good thing about it was that it led to a triple-threat match between me, Miz, and Barrett, which ended up good.

But when I got to the back afterwards, I was furious to find out that Vince had told announcer Michael Cole to call the *Highlight Reel*, and I quote, "the worst segment in *Raw* history." That pissed me off big time, and after I blew up on poor Cole for merely repeating what our boss had told him to say, I confronted Vince. He made it clear to me that he thought the segment was rotten, and when I told him that it was doomed from the start because of the awkward concept and the poor writing, he got mad.

"Well, dammit, Chris, if you ever get something handed to you that you think sucks, you need to come discuss it with me so we can change it and make it better!"

He was absolutely right and that's what I've done ever since.

When I was starting my program with Dean Ambrose in 2016, I had a myriad of ideas about how to make the storyline more exciting. So at a *Raw* in St. Louis, I went into Vince's office to sell those ideas—and myself—to him, the first of which dealt with a potted plant.

That's right, I said a potted plant.

Earlier that year, I had done a *Highlight Reel* with Ambrose and Roman Reigns and as we were writing the segment, we were laughing about the decline in quality of the *Highlight Reel*'s production values over the years.

Back in its glory days in the mid-2000s, the *Reel* set included a large carpet painted with a silhouette of the classic Jericho pose in an eye-catching array of psychedelic colors and an obscenely expensive Jeritron 5000 hanging from the ceiling, all bookended by a matching pair of Salvador Dali–looking set pieces that gave the whole set the exact neoclassical bohemian vibe I was looking for.

By 2016, it had been reduced to a plain black carpet, a dilapidated Jeritron on a rickety stand, and a pair of bar stools straight out of Moe's Tavern. As a result, Ambrose joked that he should bring a potted plant to the ring to spruce the place up a bit. It was a subtle detail that thousands of fans picked up on and commented about on Twitter, even leading to someone (it wasn't me) creating the twitter account of @JerichosPottedPlant.

Over the next few months on every *Highlight Reel*, I made sure to include a potted plant as part of the set, because in the back of my mind I envisioned eventually smashing it over somebody's head. I even pitched the idea of breaking it over AJ Styles's face before WrestleMania, which would force him to wear an eye-patch for the big match. Vince didn't like that idea, but when I suggested shattering it over Ambrose's noggin (oh, the irony) he approved it wholeheartedly.

So I laid out a plan where Ambrose would beat me in our first encounter at the Payback PPV, then I would break the plant over his head the next night, leading to a hospital stay that would cause him to miss *Smackdown*. (Miffed Author's note: One thing I hated was when the writers named the weed "Mitch the Potted Plant." It took away from the seriousness of the beatdown and made the fans think it was cute to make memes and post tweets about how I murdered the perennial, rather than focus on the fact that I had put Ambrose in the hospital.)

I also pitched another idea I'd been sitting on for years. Ever since I debuted my light-up jacket at the beginning of 2012, it had become a Jericho trademark—a late-career reinvention that made me stand out and had become an iconic part of my character. In the five years I'd been wearing the jackets (there are four in total), nobody had ever touched, threatened, or messed with them in any way. That's why I thought it was high time that somebody did.

However, I didn't really want to destroy a garment that I'd paid five figures of my own hard-earned cash for. Fortunately, after wearing it for years on TV, I noticed there were always fans in the crowd wearing their own light-up jackets. Some of them were homemade and cheap looking, but others were actually pretty good. I did some digging and found out that a company out of India was making replica "Chris Jericho Celebrity Light-Up Jackets" and selling them for the low, low price of four hundred bucks, much cheaper than the ten thousand dollars I'd paid for the original.

They looked so much like the real deal that during a tour of Australia when my jacket was barely lighting up and finally died completely, I almost sent one of our security guys out to borrow one of the replicas from a Jerichoholic in the crowd. Then I nixed the idea. I mean, Paul Stanley would never ask a fan to lend him a replica KISS costume to wear onstage, would he? So instead, I had my opponent Bray Wyatt go to the ring and cut a promo threatening to beat up a fan in the front row. My music interrupted him, and I ran in to save the day and clean house with no jacket required (and I ain't talkin' about Phil Collins).

I loved the concept of somebody destroying the jacket, so I ordered one of the replicas for four hundred bucks and kept it in my closet waiting for the right time to use it. When I started the program with Ambrose, I knew that with his quirkiness and lunatic fringe gimmick, he would be the perfect guy to destroy it. I proposed the idea to Vince as a way for Dean extract his revenge for me smashing the pot over his head, and after smartly selling the concept—and once again myself—the boss signed off on that too.

One of the writers then came up with the idea of me putting Ambrose in a straight-jacket as revenge for him destroying my property, and since I was on a roll I pitched that as well. Another homerun!

Then came the big one.

When Ambrose and head writer Dave Kapoor and I were trying to figure out what kind of gimmick match we could have as the blow-off to the feud at the Extreme Rules PPV, we didn't really have much. A straight-jacket match seemed lame, a paddy wagon match would be boring, and cage matches and ladder matches seemed too played out. We were planning on a self-explanatory Extreme Rules match, but that was given to AJ Styles and Roman Reigns instead, so we were left holding the bag. We put our heads together and came up with the idea of the first-ever Asylum match, a cage match with various weaponry hanging off the sides. We loved the idea of involving the variety of plunder that we could use to whack each other with at any time.

I knew that Vince was a sucker for the "first ever" tagline and with that in mind, I began my spiel. When I mentioned that the cage would have multiple weapons involved, Vince mumbled, "I should've known a normal cage match wouldn't be enough for you two." I ignored his comment and kept right on pitching.

I went through the basic rules and the design (painting the cage black was Ambrose's idea) and then hit him with my closing line, that it would be the "FIRST EVER" Asylum match. Vince smiled knowingly and approved it on the spot. We shook hands and I poured myself a coffee, because as Alec Baldwin says, coffee is for closers only.

We discussed our thoughts on what kinds of weapons would be used (I wanted a chainsaw that Dean would cut the top rope in half and choke me with, but Vince declined). Then I brought up the possibility of thumbtacks. Vince laughed and said, "That's not gonna happen."

I didn't figure he'd go for it, but I knew Dean wanted to try to get them approved because he had planned to use them in his street fight against Brock Lesnar at WrestleMania 32 a few months earlier. However, Brock wasn't too keen on the concept and the idea was quickly dropped. I, on the other hand, had no issue with using the tacks, since the plan was for me to beat Dean at the PPV and then challenge Roman Reigns for the title. Therefore, if the tacks were allowed, Ambrose was the one who would have to do the hibbity-dibbity in them, not me.

Over the next few weeks, the angle unfolded exactly as we had pitched, leading to some unforgettable moments (the destruction of my jacket was awesome, and instead of just wearing one of my other three light-up jackets to the ring, I switched over to the scarf). We were gearing up for the monumental Asylum blow-off match, when I got a text from Ambrose telling me that Vince had approved the tacks. I was totally surprised, but also excited because I knew it would lead to an unforgettable image when Dean took that tack bump.

But a funny thing happened on the way to the Asylum. Vince had changed his mind (what a surprise) and decided to make the returning Seth Rollins the new challenger to Roman Reigns's WWE Championship instead of me. As a result, the change was made for Ambrose to win the Asylum match, which made sense since it was "his" creation. But that meant that if anyone was going to take the tack bump . . . it had to be me.

But why would I, an established veteran with seemingly nothing left to prove, take that diabolical bump? Well, Constant

Reader, pull up a chair under the learning tree (Dusty Rhodes™) and let me explain to you a little sumpin' sumpin' about wrestling psychology.

Vince hadn't allowed a thumbtack bump in over a decade, which meant the majority of our fans had never seen such a barbaric spectacle before. And let's be honest, the whole concept of falling onto a bed of sharp objects that pierce your skin and leave you bleeding like a human pincushion is pretty fuckin' barbaric. Like feeding Christians to the lions—type stuff. Therefore, the concept of the tack bump had to be protected and sold like it was the absolute worst, most painful thing that could ever happen to a WWE superstar, and I'll tell you why.

No matter how much of a wrestling fan you are, you'll never really know how it feels to take a body slam or a suplex. You can guess how much pain you would be in, but you'll never TRULY know for sure. Therefore, when you see your heroes take this type of punishment on TV, it's never going to resonate with you in a realistic way.

However, EVERYBODY knows what it feels like to get stuck by a sharp object, whether it's a shot at the doctors or a bee sting. And as we all know, it really hurts. No matter your age, rank, or serial number, everyone's reaction to the prick of a needle is the same.

"I don't wanna get that shot because it's going to hurt when that needle goes into my skin!"

In the case of the tack bump, if you take the pain of a sole doctor's needle and multiply it by fifty, I guarantee there isn't one normal human being on the planet who would willingly allow themselves to be put in that situation.

However, pro wrestlers aren't normal human beings, and I'm not a normal pro wrestler. All that the critics and fans said after the match was "Jericho has nothing to prove and at forty-five years old did not need to take that bump!" Well, guess what—they were all wrong because I did need to take that bump.

Because that is what was best for the match.

If Ambrose took the bump and then went on to beat me, the whole point (pun intended) of using the tacks would've been wasted. It would insinuate to the fans that the tacks really didn't hurt and it was just another stunt in a show filled with dozens of them.

Uh-uh . . . not on my watch.

Much like a musician who plays what fits best for the *song* rather than showing off (think Phil Rudd in AC/DC), I knew that I would have to take the damn bump in the tacks and get pinned directly after, not because I wanted to but because it made the most sense for the story of the match.

It was also what was best for Dean Ambrose, because after months of being referred to as the lunatic fringe (and I ain't talkin' about Tom Cochrane) he hadn't done anything all that loony. But now he would be known as the psycho who dumped his opponent in a pile of thumbtacks and laughed about it after.

Honestly, I kind of got off on the idea of taking the fall, because after being in the business for twenty-five years I'd never taken a thumbtack bump before. I'd also never gotten hit with a fluorescent lightbulb or had my head stuck into a bucket filled with piranhas, but at least this made sense and put over my opponent in a way others hadn't.

I made up my mind I was going to do it and that was that. Plus, in the grand Jericho tradition of always selling myself, I knew that because the bump hadn't been done in so long, it would be one of the most memorable parts of the show and be talked about for years after. That in turn would up my profile, my fan base, and my status. See, selling yourself isn't always as simple as just picking up the phone . . . sometimes you gotta get slammed into some thumbtacks to get what you want, yo!

The Asylum match itself was kind of plodding, but when Dean grabbed a velvet bag out of a bucket hanging from the top of the cage and poured the contents into the middle of the ring, the sold-out crowd in Newark, New Jersey, gave a fifteen-thousand-person collective gasp . . . which is exactly what we were hoping for. We teased the bump a few times over the next few minutes, with each of us narrowly getting out of harm's way until I eventually locked the walls onto Dean. The crowd roared in approval, until Dean escaped by giving me a few well-placed kendo stick shots.

I turned the tide with a couple of barbed wire two-by-four shots into his abdomen and then attempted to give him a Codebreaker. However, he caught me in midair, turned to his right, and power bombed me right into the hundreds of shiny silver thumbtacks.

When I landed, I thought of Leonardo DiCaprio in *Titanic* talking about jumping into water that was so cold that "it hits you like a thousand knives stabbing you all over your body. You can't breathe. You can't think about anything but the pain." That pretty much nails (or should I say "tacks"?) how I felt—I couldn't breathe with all the pain shooting through my body. It wasn't a deep agony that would be long lasting, but more of a steady throbbing that felt like dozens of bees stinging me simultaneously.

I rose up out of the tack bath, screaming in torment with my arms outstretched in a hardcore Jesus Christ pose just as somebody snapped a picture. That photo ended up being used in hundreds of hilarious and clever memes over the next few weeks, with my faves being me jumping in the air with the Beatles in 1964, getting shot out of a cannon at a circus, being chased by Hitchcock's birds, and rocking out in the back of the car with the *Wayne's World* gang.

But the mirth of the memes aside, the worst part was trying to stand up after landing on my back. I felt like a turtle trying to turn over, as I couldn't plant my hand down anywhere to push my body up, due to the pounding prick of my new tacky friends. I couldn't bend my legs either, because I had so many of the little fuckers in the waistline of my street-fighting jeans (it was an Extreme Rules match after all) that I was afraid they would stab me and add to my increasing collection of piercings.

I shuffled/rolled around until I was able to get to my knees, all the while screaming uncontrollably to sell the severity of the bump, and then turned into Ambrose's dirty deeds DDT finish. As I took the move, I put my hands up to protect my face and while I succeeded in not having any of the tacks stick into my mug, three of the little bastards poked through the palm of my hand.

Let me tell you THAT led to some really serious pain.

I felt like a lion with three splinters in his paw, crying and writhing in agony as I rolled over so Dean could pin me. In the process, I had to arch my lower back up off the mat to avoid getting stabbed by the renegade tacks still residing in my britches.

The crowd popped huge when he got the win and he left the ring the triumphant hero who proved he was indeed the lunatic fringe he claimed to be. After all, he had barbarically brutalized (great thrash metal album title) his hated rival in a way nobody else had in over a decade.

Meanwhile, I was left alone in the ring with sixty-eight tacks sticking out of my bleeding body, with the three most painful ones jammed into my hand. That trio of pushpins was giving me so much agony that I decided to make sure the world knew they were there. I looked towards the camera, whimpering pathetically in torment, and held my wounded hand next to my face with the palm towards the lens, giving the world a close-up of my anguish.

And why did I go out of my way to get that shot on camera?

Because (say it with me now, kids) I was selling myself!

EPILOGUE

After having a total of sixty-eight tacks removed from my back, shoulders, and elbows by the WWE doctors and trainers (every one of them caught on camera, of course), I went to the dressing room to take off my boots. I sat down, but recoiled instantly when my ass hit the bench as another flash of torture sliced through my lower body like a Lilliputian spear. I stood up gingerly and pulled down my pants, twisting my neck to try and see my own rear end (which isn't easy, let me tell you) and there it was, the parting gift of the Asylum: one last thumbtack sticking out of my left buttock.

Change that number to sixty-nine, tacks of Jericho . . . stick 'em in, maaan!

EPILOGUE PART 2

A few days ago as of this writing, I was sitting at the pool at the hotel where the entire company was staying for WrestleMania 33, when Ambrose approached me and showed me a picture on his phone. Unbeknownst to me, a toy company had just released an Asylum match playset complete with a breakable Mitch the Potted Plant. So despite the fact that critics HATED the first Asylum match, I'm sure they'll be happy to know that since there is now a playset of the structure, there will probably be another one.

You're welcome!

CHAPTER 16

THE
SHEP
GORDON
PRINCIPLE

YOU NEVER KNOW
WHO'S WATCHING YOU

Every breath you take, every move you make,
every bond you break, I'll be watching you . . .
—THE POLICE, "EVERY BREATH YOU TAKE"

As I was writing this book, my dad came to visit us in Florida, and one night we were talking about life in general. He commented that if you wanted to succeed, you needed to put forth your best effort at all times, because "you just never who's watching you." It was a great point, one that applies to this lexicon perfectly. It was another great piece of advice from my father and my mentor, but when he said it, I had already written the chapter explaining the Ted Irvine Principle. However, this new nugget of advice was too good not to use, so I decided to incorporate it under the banner of The Shep Gordon Principle instead.

If you're not familiar with the name Shep Gordon, then you need to check out *Supermensch,* the excellent documentary about his life, directed by Mike Myers. *Mensch* is a Yiddish word for "a person of integrity and honor," and that describes Shep to a tee. He's a universally regarded great person whose pedigree in show business is legendary. He's been Alice Cooper's manager for over forty-five years and has also guided or assisted the careers of Blondie, Anne Murray, Raquel Welch, Teddy Pendergrass, Luther Vandross, Johnny Depp, Sammy Hagar, and even the Beatles. He's also one of the nicest people I've ever met and most people who know him feel the same way.

But as illustrious as Shep's pedigree is, I wasn't familiar with him until I watched his documentary while touring with Fozzy in Europe in the fall of 2015. As soon as I saw the film, I instantly liked this capricious gent and spread the word about him and the movie to anyone and everyone who would listen.

Fast-forward a few months to Valentine's Day 2016 and I was back with the WWE, getting ready for a matinee show in Fresno, when suddenly I got a text from Paul Stanley.

WHAT ARE YOU DOING TONIGHT? MY WIFE IS SICK, SO DO YOU WANNA COME WITH ME TO CLIVE DAVIS'S GRAMMY PARTY?

Was he ribbing me? Of course I wanted to go!

Clive Davis is one of the biggest record executives in history and his parties are legendary. This was THE place to be the night before the Grammys and was almost impossible to get into. But now that I was invited, I had to figure out what I was going to wear.

After searching through the various vests, scarves, and suit jackets that were rolled up at the bottom of my suitcase, I was able to put together a decent little ensemble (although it could've used a quick ironing), and after my match I quickly showered and took off for the three-hour drive back to Los Angeles.

The plan was to meet Paul at the Beverly Hilton at 7 p.m. sharp, and when I pulled up to the hotel it was a madhouse. Fans and reporters were everywhere, trying catch a glimpse of the icons of pop culture history that were walking through the metal detectors at the front of the venue.

I arrived a few minutes early, so I waited at the bar and had a Yeah Boy to relax, as this was a pretty high-class affair and I wasn't sure if I would know anybody else besides Paul. A few minutes later he arrived and we stood in line waiting to go through the metal detectors leading into the ballroom. He gave me my pass and we made small talk for a few minutes, until I noticed that blues guitar legend Buddy Guy was standing right in front of us. When I pointed him out to Paul, he grabbed his iPhone and asked Buddy if he could take a quick picture. It was cool to see one of my rock 'n' roll heroes fanboying out and getting a picture with a hero of his own.

Once we got through the craziness of the security line and the scrum of the red carpet (I was done in about ten minutes, while Paul took over thirty . . . it was definitely more his crowd than mine), we walked into another bar area and that's when I realized just how many very important people were at this shindig.

Within ten minutes, Paul had introduced me to Suzanne Somers, Sly Stallone, Desmond Child, Diane Warren, and Taylor Hawkins. I also saw a myriad of old acquaintances, including Dave Grohl (you owe me a drink, dude!), Sammy Hagar, Gene Simmons ("you are a powerful and attractive man"), Alice Cooper, and David Foster, while Chris Rock, Jamie Foxx, Ringo Starr, Gwen Stefani, Rod Stewart, Michael J. Fox (who was sitting right behind me the whole time but I couldn't get up the nerve to say hi), Bette Midler, Irving Azoff, Khloe Kardashian, P Diddy, and dozens of other A-listers milled about. If it seems like I'm name-dropping again, it's because I am . . . so watch your toes.

There was also a frail-looking bushy-haired kid who seemed like he was about twelve years old walking around with an ill-fitting tuxedo and a goofy grin. He looked confused and out of place . . . then I realized he was Harry Styles from One Direction.

Paul and I hung around until the bar closed and we were walking into the main room for the dinner and entertainment portion of the party, when we ran into Shep Gordon himself. I was happy to meet him and I mentioned I'd seen his movie and dug his infectious laugh. He was very cordial with his reply; we shook hands and went our separate ways.

A few minutes later, Paul and I got to our assigned table (like at a wedding) and I noticed that they had put all the rockers together in the back of the room. How's this for a lineup: Alice Cooper, Gene Simmons, Shannon Tweed, Paul, Chad Kroeger, Avril LaVigne, a random lesbian couple, and sitting beside me in an act of pure happenstance . . . Shep Gordon.

There were some serious road dogs in that group, a fact put into perspective by Alice when he queried, "Can you imagine the total amount of road miles traveled at this table?" It was a great point and I stopped counting in my head when I reached twenty million. Hell, I was probably around four million myself.

Shep and I hit it off instantly and after a few minutes of small talk about where we lived (he was based in Maui), we decided we wanted a drink. The only problem was the bar was now closed (what kind of a rock 'n' roll party was this anyway?), and only wine was available at that point. Either Clive ran a pretty tight ship at his Grammy parties, or he was just a Grumpus who didn't want his guests having too much fun. Sensing that neither of us were big fans of rules, Shep and I paid no attention to the abandoned bar and flagged down our waiter, a friendly-looking older Latino dude with an engaging smile.

"Excuse me, sir, is there any chance you can grab a couple of vodka and cranberries for us?" Shep asked him politely. He nodded his head with a smile and in a few minutes returned with four stiff cocktails.

"Here you go, boss," the guy said cheerfully. I tipped him twenty bucks and Shep and I toasted each other, as we turned our attention to the stage at the front of the room.

The show started and throughout the course of the night, we were treated to live performances from the surviving members of Nirvana with Beck on vocals (it was incredible and they should do a tour), Barry Manilow, Earth, Wind & Fire, Chicago, Carly Simon, and Fetty Wap. Then Melissa Etheridge did a tribute to the recently departed Glenn Frey with a rendition of the Eagles' "Take It Easy," which didn't turn out too well as the melody of the song was way out of her raspy range. But the crowd gave her a standing ovation anyway, and even though it wasn't really deserved, her heart was in the right place, so I rose out of the chair along with the rest of my table.

Gene was clapping his hands with a frozen grin and when he caught my eye, he whispered through clenched teeth, "Well, that was the shits." I almost spit out my cocktail.

Paul was just as funny, throwing out quips and lines the entire show.

"Hey, Paul, why is Nancy Pelosi here?"

"I think she's a member of Heart," he deadpanned with perfect comic delivery.

What was even more comical was the appearance of the waiter every fifteen minutes with another four cocktails, whether Shep and I asked for them or not. But we kept tipping him, so he kept coming back saying, "Here you go, boss," every time until we literally had a half dozen drinks each in front of us.

I was starting to get self-conscious, as it seemed that everybody else at the table was either a recovering alcoholic or a teetotaler, making Shep and me look like Keith Moon and Bon Scott in 1977.

"We really didn't ask for all of these drinks," I said to Paul guiltily after another delivery from Boss, as if he really gave a fuck. He had been in KISS for over forty years and had seen and done it all I'm sure, so I doubt a table full of vodka made him bat a star-painted eye. But I still felt weird when Boss returned with another couple highballs.

"Why does he keep coming back so quickly, Shep?"

"I think it's because we keep giving him money. I just tipped him another two hundred bucks."

We did some quick math and realized that between the two of us, Boss had made almost five hundred bucks in less than two hours. No wonder he was so punctual with his service.

"I think we might have just adopted him," I said. "We are going to have to share custody. He can live with you in Hawaii during the week, then I get him on the weekends in Tampa."

It was nonstop laughter that night and one of those froot times when you hit it off with somebody instantly. I was only aware of Shep because of his movie, plus he was twenty-five years my senior and I was pretty sure he'd never heard of me, but it didn't matter; a kindred spirit is a kindred spirit.

Finally, Shep and his date got up to leave, but he handed me a disheveled business card that was probably printed in 1969 and told me to look him up if I was ever coming to Hawaii.

"As a matter of fact, Shep, I'm planning on taking my family to Maui this summer. Do you think you might be able to point me in the right direction of somewhere cool to stay?"

"Yes I can. Email me tomorrow and we will figure it out."

I pocketed his card and shook his hand. A few minutes later Paul and Gene left as well. So I hung out a little while longer looking for Ringo to hear him pee or whatever, but he had left too. With nobody else to hang with, I finished off one of the remaining six drinks on the table and walked out the door, hip-checking that little shit Harry Styles along the way.

The next day I emailed Shep and was amazed when I got his reply a few hours later: "If you are looking for a place to stay in Maui, why don't you just stay at my place? I have a guest house with plenty of room and if I'm in town I'll even cook you a meal or two."

I couldn't believe his offer and I knew exactly what his guest-house looked like because I'd seen it in the documentary—it was real and it was spectacular!

It took me a while to convince Jess that I wasn't crazy for accepting an offer to take my family to stay for a week at a stranger's house. However, once I showed her the *Supermensch* movie and she read the litany of emails from Nancy Meola (Shep's amazing personal assistant) offering to book any activity we wanted to do, she realized it was a once in a lifetime opportunity and not a scene out of *The King of Comedy*.

In the end she was glad we went, because it definitely was the vacation of a lifetime. All the wonderful things we saw and experienced in Maui are too numerous to describe in this chapter and will have to be told in a separate book, but suffice it to say it was a family vacation after which Jess, Ash, Cheyenne, Sierra and I will never, EEEVVVEEERRR be the same again. And we owe it all to Shep Gordon, a man who extended us the full use of his home for a week, after only knowing me for ninety minutes.

But here's the moral of the story.

On the last day of our vacation, Shep agreed to do an interview for *Talk Is Jericho*. After regaling me with incredible stories from his forty-five-year career for over an hour (his tale about John and Yoko shaving their heads so the aliens would know it was time to come take them away was a personal favorite of mine), I thanked him for sharing his home with me and for allowing my family to be a part of his incredible world. He reciprocated and told me how much he enjoyed having us there for the week, which was nice to hear, but it was the bomb he dropped on me next that hit me hardest.

"It's been great to hang with you . . . I've been a fan of yours for a while."

What? A fan of mine from what? I knew Shep had worked with the WWE briefly in the '80s when Alice Cooper appeared at WrestleMania 2, but he didn't seem the type who was keeping up with the business in 2016.

"I was at the Golden God Awards a few years ago where you hosted and Alice played. I thought you were excellent. You did a great job of relating to the audience even though you came from a different world. It really impressed me and I was happy to finally meet you at Clive's party. I'm a fan of yours."

His statement was a total shock, Constant Reader, because I had no idea Shep had ever seen my work . . . which proves you just never know who's watching.

I always give my all in whatever I do and that included hosting the Golden God Awards four years in a row (all described at length in my third literary masterpiece, *The Best in the World*). But because Shep enjoyed my work the year he was there, it laid the foundation for a tremendous experience for me, and my family. It also opened the door to me being able to call one of the most genuine and interesting people on the planet my friend.

Aloha, Shep!

HOOKING UP with Mr. Gordon was a great moment for me and my family, but years earlier, impressing an unseen source didn't just land me a vacation, it landed me a job.

In the summer of 1995, I had been wrestling for five years and had made a good name for myself in Mexico and Japan, but I'd still received no bites from the big leagues in the States. It bothered me, but I was still enjoying myself working for WAR and was about have the biggest match of my career in the Tokyo Sumo Hall against Ultimo Dragon for the Junior Heavyweight title.

There was a big buzz for the bout and the sold-out crowd gave us a great reaction for one of my best matches to date. What I didn't know was that Hardcore Legend/Mick Foley was in the crowd that night and even though we hadn't really met, he was so impressed with my work that he spoke to ECW head honcho Paul Heyman about bringing me in and raved about me.

That planted the seed in Heyman's head to book me in ECW, and even though it took him eight months, he eventually brought me in with some serious fanfare (and I ain't talkin' about The Elder). On top of that, Chris Benoit got a hold of a tape of the Dragon match and passed it on to Jimmy Hart at WCW, who in turn passed it on to Paul Orndorff, who liked it enough to leave it on bossman Eric Bischoff's desk. I'm not sure Eric ever watched it, but the chatter about me was enough that he pretty much hired me on sight when I met him at the World Wrestling Peace Festival in Los Angeles in the summer of 1996. The word of mouth spread by people I hadn't met was enough to finally get me into the big leagues of WCW.

The other side to all this, however, is that not knowing who's watching can also work against you, ya dig?

One night in Pittsburgh in 2004, I was in Vince's office going over a promo for Raw when the dark matches started. A certain performer who'd had a decent run in the company a few years prior (whom I'll call Bobby Baby to protect his ego), had just been rehired after some sort of hiatus and was having a few nontelevised matches to try out a new character. Unfortunately, it wasn't working and when Vince (who was already in a surly mood) saw him struggling through a dismal match, he flipped his toupee.

"Why the hell is this guy in my ring? Who rehired him? Look at this . . . he's the shits and I don't want to see him again."

Needless to say, we never saw poor Bobby Baby in a WWE ring again, and I'll bet nobody told him why he was getting let go. So now you know, Bobby. I'm sure you can figure out who you are.

BEING SCOUTED without my knowledge also led me to having one of my most cherished experiences, playing a song for Lemmy at his seventieth birthday party.

I was over in Europe on the last leg of the Do You Wanna Start a War tour in December 2015, when I got an email from longtime

Motörhead manager Todd Singerman, inviting me to Lemmy's milestone bash at the famous Whiskey a Go Go on the Sunset Strip. Lem had been suffering from some health issues over the past few years, so I was happy that he had made it to seventy and was honored to be included in the plans. But after having just been on tour for almost a month, I didn't think I'd be able to take another day away from home to travel to Los Angeles.

Over the next few days Todd kept asking me if I'd come, saying the party wouldn't be the same without me and that Lemmy really wanted me there. I'd forged a pretty decent friendship with him over the years, including being invited over to his apartment for him to do my podcast and show me his massive collection of World War II memorabilia. We had an awesome time and he was a tremendous interview, which was the opposite of what I'd heard about him. He liked talking to me I think, because we were into a lot of the same things: the Beatles and the Stones, *Fawlty Towers,* bad jokes, and Grey Goose vodka, his new drink of choice after being forced to give up his beloved whiskey for health reasons. ("I'm sure his liver knew the difference," Alice Cooper quipped when we discussed Lem on *Talk Is Jericho*.)

After a great ninety-minute chat, we spent another couple hours drinking vodka, smoking cigarettes (I hadn't smoked in years, but when the legendary Lemmy offers you a butt, you damn well have one!) and hearing intricate descriptions and stories about every knife, spoon, medal, sword, sash, flag, and gun hanging from his wall. He even had Eva Braun's cutlery and an actual lighter owned by Hitler himself in his collection. I don't know what happened to that assemblage after his passing, but it was so extensive and impressive, it needs to be in a museum somewhere.

I could've stayed and hung out with him all day, but I had to leave to catch a flight, so a very frail Lemmy told me to "come back anytime, I'd love to have you over again."

But I never had the chance, so when Singerman sent me yet another email asking if I could make the party and be a part of the all-star jam that was taking place, I reconsidered and said yes. I didn't know when I'd get the chance to see Lemmy again and didn't want to miss out.

The all-star jam was going to be made up of a huge collection of legendary musicians, including Billy Idol, Zakk Wylde, Sebastian Bach, Steve Jones, Gilby Clark, Doug Pinnick, Bob Kulick, Nuno Bettencourt, and Steve Vai, and I was honored to have been asked to be a part of it. I asked Todd what song I'd be singing and he told me to contact Matt Sorum, the ex–Guns N' Roses/Cult drummer who was the musical director of the jam and putting together the lineups.

Matt asked me if I wanted to sing ZZ Top's "Beer Drinkers and Hell Raisers" with Slash, Scott Ian, Charlie Benante, Rob Trujillo, and Whit Crane. I started laughing at how ridiculous my life was that I was getting to play a ZZ Top tune at Lemmy's birthday party with some of the most respected musicians in rock 'n' roll; all of whom were my friends.

The only problem was that due to my travel schedule, I had to fly in a few hours before the show, which meant I would miss rehearsals.

"No problem," Matt replied. "I've seen you play before. I came to a Fozzy gig with (Motörhead guitarist) Phil Campbell. I already know you can sing and perform, so just get there when you can."

I had no idea Sorum had ever been to a Fozzy gig and this was another example of never knowing who's got their eyes on you.

On the night of the party, the Whiskey was packed with hundreds of fans and friends of the most notorious rock 'n' roll pirate ever (you could maybe say Keith Richards, but it wasn't his birfday now, was it?). Lemmy sat above the proceedings on a large throne in the balcony, which was apropos because even as fragile and weak as he looked, he was still the KING.

The jam started and I have to admit it was pretty effin' cool to walk onstage at the world-famous Whiskey with Slash, Scott, Charlie, Rob, and Whit. I felt like I was in the most famous bar band in the world.

I walked up to the mic and said, "Hello, we are the New Faster Pussycat," which made about twelve people chuckle, and Charlie clicked us off. The band kicked in with that classic Billy Gibbons chugging riff, and Whit took the first line of the song: "If you see me walking down the line . . ." then I fell in behind him with the second: ". . . with my favorite honky-tonk in mind." We were off and rocking.

The great thing about playing with true pros is there was no rehearsal necessary to make it work. Everybody was on point and this was one of the best moments of my musical career. Trading off lines and sharing harmonies with a singer as talented as Whit Crane was an honor, even if I had to teach him the meter of the song . . . and he'd been at rehearsal! Anthrax and Fozzy had toured together, so sharing the stage with Charlie and Scott was as natural as being caught in a mosh.

But then there were the Rock & Roll Hall of Famers.

Rob Trujillo had been inducted into the Hall with Metallica, and if you didn't hear what I said, I'll repeat it.

ROB TRUJILLO IS IN METALLICA.

I made sure to spend as much time as possible whiplashing on his side of the stage and enjoying the moment, because I'm pretty sure I won't be the lead singer in Metallica any time soon. He was totally locked in with Scott and Charlie as if they had been playing together for years, which considering the lineage of their respective bands, they kind of had been.

But as good as all the other cats were that night, it was Slash who stole the show. We had been friends for years, but I got a whole new appreciation for his playing while rocking beside him as he soloed. The band had decided to do an extended break during the bridge section for Slash to rip over and he delivered each note with a slimy, dirty, reckless abandon that was oh so totally rock 'n' roll. I hung beside him and danced like Mick Jagger for an hour (or five minutes), clapping and swaying to the music and getting in his face the whole time. I'm not sure if my Ozzy/Randy, Jericho/Ward–style of interacting freaked him out because he never looked up from his axe once, but I had a fuck-ing blast anyway.

The audience seemed to dig it as well, because when the song ended they gave the New Faster Pussycat a raucous roar as we stomped off the stage. It was a night I'll never forget and even though the other guys might never write about it in THEIR books, it sure as shit belongs in mine. As a matter of fact, if I can borrow a line from the doomed quartet in *Titanic*, I'd like to say to those five dudes, "Gentlemen, it was a privilege playing with you."

Sadly, I've never seen a full video of that performance, so if somebody out there has one, please send it to me at @iamjericho on the Twittah!

After the jam ended, the birthday celebration began. Sorum introduced a tremendous video montage of dozens of musicians and celebrities wishing Lemmy a happy seventieth birthday; thanking him for all he'd done, and spinning filthy tales of his wicked sense of humor and infamous debauchery. It was an amazing tribute and I couldn't take my eyes off the screen, even though Lem couldn't seem to keep his eyes on it, as he sat on his throne reading a book the whole time.

It was classic Kilmister: hundreds of people were assembled to praise his name and he couldn't give a fuck. It reminded me of one of my favorite lines from our podcast, when I asked him how he reacted when people told him he was God.

"I'm not God . . . .God's taller," he deadpanned with a smirk.

After the video finished, I made my way over to his throne, which was surrounded by onlookers and well-wishers. I saw his girlfriend, Cheryl, (who saved my ass when I did the interview at his place by giving me a pack of AA batteries when I lost the power charger for my Zoom unit) and asked her if it was okay to say hello.

She grabbed my hand and dragged me through the pack straight to him and I was stunned to see how gaunt and pale he looked up close. I said hello and happy birthday, but when he gazed up from his book, I saw how deep his eyes were sunk into their sockets. He didn't look good.

His expression never changed when he saw me and I wasn't sure he even knew who I was. I asked him if he was having a good time and he nodded slowly, but I could tell he was over the whole thing and probably wanted to get the fuck out of there.

I didn't want to hassle him so I leaned in and gave him our favorite line from *Fawlty Towers:*

"Listen, don't mention the war! I mentioned it once but I think I got away with it . . ."

Even that classic quote didn't break Lemmy's stoic demeanor, so I decided to cut my losses and leave him alone. But before I could go, he slowly raised his hand and extended his pinky. I wasn't sure what he was doing but I didn't want to leave him hanging, so I wrapped my pinky around his and shook it up and down like a prepubescent schoolgirl making a promise. He shook it back for a few seconds, then pulled away and went back to reading his book.

I never saw him again.

Lem passed away just two weeks later, after finding out he had terminal cancer the day before. I strongly believe that when he found out his fate, he willed himself to die quickly so he wouldn't cause himself or anybody else any further pain. He went out on his own terms, the exact same way he lived his life.

I'm so grateful I made the decision to go to his party, because aside from being a part of the amazing jam, I got to see my friend one last time.

A few months after Lemmy's passing I happened to see a picture of him and Phil Campbell onstage at a gig. I'd seen hundreds of pictures of them before, but this one stood out because they were standing with their arms raised, giving each other the "pinky swear" handshake. I called Phil and asked him what the greeting was all about.

"We did that every night," he told me. "It was Lemmy's ultimate show of respect. Fans always asked him to shake pinkies but he wouldn't do it. He saved that only for the people that he really liked." Phil's words touched me and made me even happier that I'd made the trip to Los Angeles that day to pay tribute to my friend.

Thanks for everything, Lemmy. I miss you and I'll see you on the other side. Please have a Grey Goose and a cigarette waiting for me.

EPILOGUE

At the party after Lemmy's birthday video aired, I bumped into Lars Ulrich. I had no idea he was there but we always got along well and had a good talk about the party, the humor of Lemmy reading his book during the tribute, and the evening's musical entertainment.

"You guys kicked ass on 'Beer Drinkers,'" he said favorably. "That's one of Lemmy's favorite tunes . . . Motörhead even covered it back in 1980. You guys did a great job and I'm glad I got to see it."

You just never know who's watching.

CHAPTER 17

THE
RONNIE JAMES DIO
PRINCIPLE
(AKA
THE ELLSWORTH EDICT)

GIVE EVERYONE
THEIR MOMENT

We are all a star . . .
—PRINCE, "BABY I'M A STAR"

The night Fozzy played the Motörhead thirtieth anniversary show in Los Angeles, I got a nice compliment about my vocal stylings from the legendary Ronnie James Dio. He was backstage checking out our show (you never know who's watching) and by going out of his way to tell me he enjoyed my performance, he gave me a memory that will last a lifetime.

I thought it was really great of him to do that, so it didn't surprise me when I saw him signing autographs later for a group of fans hanging around the backstage door after the gig. Being nice to people seemed to be Ronnie's natural modus operandi.

After he finished signing and taking pictures for every person waiting, I asked him if he always did that.

"Yeah, I try to give people their moment, Chris. You might not remember signing an autograph or shaking a hand, but that person will never forget it. And they'll also never forget it if you blow them off."

Ronnie was absolutely right and I'm sure all of you have had brushes with people you admired that turned out well and others that ended not so great.

When I first met Hulk Hogan in the lobby of the Polo Park Inn in Winnipeg at fifteen years old, I remember him shaking my hand and asking what my name was. "Nice to meet you, Chris," Hulkster said, and I'll never forget how good it made me feel when he called me by name. Conversely, I also remember Sika the Wild Samoan (who incidentally is Roman Reigns's father) looking me in the eye and telling me to "fuck off, kid" when I asked him for an autograph.

I have to point out that even though each guy treated me completely different, they both gave me a memory that will last forever.

Now, that might sound a little strange at first, but hear me out. Hogan was gracious and accommodating, like a true baby-face should be, while Sika was rude, abrasive, and mean . . . like a true heel should be. In their different ways, both of them gave me a few seconds of their time, and provided experiences I'll never forget.

By virtue of that, I've followed Sika's lead and have the same attitude when I'm playing a heel. Whenever I'm on "WWE ground" (e.g., in an airport or at the arena before a show) and I'm playing a bad guy, I don't sign or take pictures with anybody. So if you decide to wait at baggage claim for me to autograph your Chris Jericho ice cream bar or ask for a selfie at the arena, please don't take it personally if I decline. I'm only doing my job.

If I give you Mr. Niceguy and accommodate your requests before the show, what incentive is there for you to boo me later? I never tell people to fuck off like Sika did, but if I stroll past you and say, "Sorry, I'm not signing. I'm a bad guy," I'm still giving you your moment, but in a heelish manner, which is the way it should be.

However, when I'm a babyface I go out of my way to try to sign or take pictures whenever I can. I even breached the top security of the hotel in Jeddah, Saudi Arabia, in order to spend time with some Friends of Jericho who weren't allowed into the lobby . . . because they were female.

I'd never been to Saudi before and when we arrived, I was really surprised to see how disrespected the women were in the country. They were expected to wear veils over their faces, walk a few feet behind their men, and weren't allowed to attend the WWE show. As a matter of fact, NO WOMEN ALLOWED was printed in bold letters, right on the tickets.

That was strange to me, not just from a religious standpoint, but from a business standpoint as well. The shows were about 70 percent sold with no females of any age allowed inside, which tells me that if the girls had been permitted to buy tickets it would've been a sellout. Not to mention it was a pretty weird scenario performing in an arena filled with all men, as the cheers during the matches were deeper and less frantic than usual.

Another unusual thing about the Jeddah shows was that intermission had to start exactly at 5:55 p.m., because at 6 p.m. the show stopped so the entire crowd could go outside, face Mecca, and pray. Then twenty minutes later after the prayers were done, the crowd filed back in and the show continued.

The Muslim traditions in the country were so strict that chanting prayers were blasted over loudspeakers every morning at six across the entire city, which woke me up daily like an Allahm clock (see what I did there?) without fail. Waking up to the mantras was an eerie feeling and reminded me that I was a long way from home. Throw in the fact that there was no alcohol available anywhere (even the possession of it was punishable by public flogging). and let's just say it wasn't the most fun I've ever had on a tour.

Another thing that bothered me was the handful of female fans crowded around on the highway in front of the gate of the hotel, waiting to get a glance of their favorite WWE superstars. I was worried they would get hit by a car (or worse), but since Saudi Arabia was such a dangerous country, we had been warned not to leave the hotel premises to say hi to them. However, after seeing one of the highway girls holding up a Y2J sign as we drove by on the bus, I decided I'd had enough.

We pulled up to the lobby, but instead of walking into the hotel I took a left and marched towards the gate, determined to give those ladies their moment.

"You can't go that way," a jacked-up security guard (alcohol might've been impossible to get in the country, but it appeared steroids were quite accessible) mumbled in my direction. *Watch me*, I thought as I strolled through the opening.

The first fan I saw was a little girl about eleven years old holding a sign that read: I CAN'T WAIT TO SEE JOHN CENA! It broke my heart to know that a random viewing of John on the bus was her only chance to lay eyes on her hero. I still can't believe that in 2017 such inequality exists in the world, but seeing it up close hit me hard. I approached the mob and shook hands, took pictures, signed autographs (the girl with the Y2J sign got an extra hug), and spent as much time as I could with the small group of devotees, trying to give them a special moment I knew they wouldn't forget.

This isn't an attitude that should only be limited to celebrities either; it can apply to everyone in all walks of life. If you're in an influential position, compliment the people around you. Give them a smile and a pat on the back if they've done a good job, and let them know you appreciate them. This extends even more to your children—give them a hug and tell them you love them as much as you can on a daily basis. Praise them when they do good in school and don't blow up when they make a mistake.

Having a positive attitude solves problems and helps make difficult situations better.

Another seemingly small detail that makes a huge difference
is to make an effort to remember people's NAMES. Full disclo-
sure: I'm terrible at this and there are people I've worked with
in the WWE for years whose names I'm still not completely sure
of. It's an awful thing to say, but don't think I'm a total muttonhead, because I was never formally introduced to some of them
in the first place. Whenever you go into a new environment and
meet dozens of people in the first few days, it's hard to catch everybody's name, right? I think Elaine Benes's idea that everyone
should wear name tags is actually pretty smart, as calling someone "dude" or "man" for years because you don't know their actual moniker is pretty embarrassing.

The most embarrassing thing of all, however, is calling someone by the wrong name, especially if they don't correct you. I
once did a whole interview with Zach Myers from Shinedown
thinking that his last name was Evans. I was making Evansville,
Indiana, and "Good Times" jokes for an hour, until I realized my
mistake.

"Why didn't you tell me I was messing up your name, dude?"

"Because I didn't want to make you feel bad!"

I know the feeling, as I once spent the summer of '86 working
as a department store stockboy covering up my name tag because the old lady in housewares thought my name was Dave.

"How are you, Dave? Do you know that my grandson's name
is Dave? It's such a nice name!"

"Thank you, Mrs. Bobski . . ."

I was too ashamed to correct her, so I just went with it for
three months.

Something as simple as calling people by their names goes
a long way, even if you're the drummer for the biggest heavy
metal band in the world.

In February of 2013, Fozzy were fortunate enough to be invited on the Soundwave tour in Australia, headlined by the

mighty Metallica. Soundwave was a traveling festival with some forty-odd bands playing five stadium shows across the country over the course of ten days. It was a lot of fun because it was like summer camp: you saw the same people for a week and a half straight, all of us traveling together and staying at the same hotels. By the end of the run everyone had pretty much gotten to know each other, but when we first arrived nobody really knew who was who for the most part, until Metallica had their pre–opening night barbeque bash in Brisbane.

You see, a few days before the tour started, each band's tour manager received an email invite to the soiree, welcoming every musician on the tour to hang out with Metallica and party on their dime.

"As if James Hetfield is going to be hanging around talking to everybody," Fozzy drummer Frank Fontsere mocked as the bus pulled up to the stadium concourse where the bash was taking place. Five seconds later, he stopped in his tracks when Papa Het himself greeted him as we got off the bus. James wasn't the only Metallicat in attendance either, as Lars, Rob, and Kirk (who mentioned to me later that 'Tallica band attendance was mandatory) were also milling around, pressing the flesh, and introducing themselves to various band members, some of whom were in such a state of starstruck stupor they could hardly string six words together. You have to remember that a lot of these guys were meeting their heroes for the first time, so to be touring with Metallica AND hanging around with them was leaving them helpless . . . in the best possible way.

The spread was impressive, but James and I only picked through the food, trying gamely to stick to the caveman diet he had turned me on to a few years prior. We had a conversation about '80s doom metal pioneers Trouble who had no real image, and compared that to the image of the modern-day rock star. It seemed that every musician at the party under the age of thirty sported neck tattoos, cut-off skinny jeans, an aviator haircut with a handlebar moustache, and a tank top with the sides cut low to seemingly accentuate their developing man boobs.

"Man, these guys look like posers," James sneered. "If I was starting a band today most of these guys wouldn't even get in the door."

We continued mocking the youth of the day like a pair of heavy metal Statler and Waldorfs until it was time for James to go mingle elsewhere. I wandered over to Lars, who was holding court with a bunch of kids so green they looked like Keebler elves.

The rookies stood transfixed, mumbling stilted answers to Lars's questions, but even though they were nervous beyond words, he handled it like a pro and was able to maintain a decent conversation. Lars looked them in the eye as they spoke and showed bona fide interest in what they were saying, which is one of his most endearing qualities. After listening to him talk for a few minutes, I noticed he knew some of the guys' names and later asked him why, since it was obvious he'd never met them or heard of their bands before.

"When we decided to have this party, I had my assistant put together a book with pictures of all the bands on the tour and their names written underneath," he explained. "I looked through it for days hoping to remember some of the names, or at least be able to put a face to a band."

I thought that was pretty fucking cool that Lars would put in that type of effort, because he sure didn't have to. He was focused on giving some people their moments and that showed what a classy guy he was. As a matter of fact, the entire Metallica organization was pretty classy, and I learned a lot about how to treat and respect our support bands. Inspired by the effort Lars showed with his book, I now try to extend the same effort when getting to know the other bands on tour with Fozzy. I always try to have a chat with the members, give them our leftover beer or dressing room catering, and make it a point to watch their sets as much as I can during a tour. A little genuine attention goes a long way.

I also decided to employ more of a Lars-style effort when it came to the extras backstage at WWE events as well. At every television taping, there are usually a half dozen or so local wrestlers who turn up with the hopes of having a tryout and getting booked on the show. You can spot them a mile away, standing nervously against the wall, dressed in suits and trying not to bother anybody, hoping against hope that Vince McMahon himself will walk by and go, "Wow, you're exactly what I've been looking for! I'm making you world champion tomorrow!"

While that has yet to happen, once in a while an extra will be selected for an on-air role, usually as a security guard or backstage random. And on rare occasions a local will end up with a match on *Raw* . . . and that's how I became a fan of one James Ellsworth.

I first saw James wandering around backstage confusedly at the *Raw* tapings in Pittsburgh in July of 2016. With all due respect, at first glance wrestling seemed like an odd choice for him, as let's just say he didn't exactly have the classic wrestler look.

He was about five foot six with a body that resembled a pale Gumby, with no real muscle tone to speak of. His dyed canary-blond hair was slicked back against his scalp like a villain from a 1930s caper movie, with a large, smudged Offspring monster logo tattooed on his shoulder.

But his most (or least) distinguishing feature was his apparent lack of chin.

Now when I say "lack of chin" I'm not saying it was small or covered by facial hair. I'm saying he literally had no chin . . . like it had been blown off in the war. That particular peculiarity earned him the creative nickname "No Chin" among the boys in the locker room.

Now, as much as his physical features would in theory seem to work against No Chin in the WWE big picture, on that night they worked totally in his favor. It was the first *Raw* after the 2016 brand extension, and in an effort to change the look of the show from previous Monday nights, Vince decided to bring squash matches back.

A squash match meant that a local guy would be pitted against an established superstar, get zero offense in, and lose in a minute or two. These type of matches were a staple of WWE programming in the '80s, but had disappeared over the last twenty years, even though they were a good way to get fans familiar with new characters, their gimmicks, and their finishing moves. With that in mind, it made sense to bring them back, and the first squash match in the WWE in years pitted No Chin Ellsworth against the gargantuan six foot ten, 375-pound Braun Strowman.

After seeing Ellsworth backstage during the day, I thought his size and strange look would make him the perfect man for the job (pun intended), as his lack of stature and build made Strowman look even more impressive than he already was. Since I'd never seen James before, I figured he was just some green dude who'd been training for a few weeks and would be out of the business in a few months. But boy was I wrong . . . it turns out there was a lot I didn't know about James Ellsworth.

For example, I didn't know that Vince had decided to give him a pre-match interview and once I heard it, the chinless, child-sized Pidgeotto became my new favorite wrestler.

In a shaky, terrified voice Ellsworth talked about having hope that he could pull off the upset on Strowman. because "any man with two hands has a fighting chance." (Was he saying if you only have one hand you're doomed? Tell that to Luke Skywalker, No Chin!). I was surprised that this jobber had gotten some mic time, and even more astonished when he nailed his promo. He took his time with a good delivery and really got across the sense that he was scared shitless. At that point, I realized he wasn't as green as I'd thought—he knew what he was doing.

He also did a great job of getting jobbed, as Braun brutally destroyed him and finished him off with a vicious reverse chokeslam. It was comical how easily Strowman jerked him up into the air, giving the crowd a bird's-eye view of the Ellster's

"Oh shit" face and one-armed gingerbread man pose. The whole segment was a gas to watch and apparently Vince felt the same way, as he found James after and personally congratulated him for a job well done.

I gained a ton of respect for James after watching his performance, and had to smile when I thought about the day he was having. He shows up at the arena and against all odds randomly gets booked to have a match on *Raw* (something that thousands of pro wrestlers dream about daily), gets promo time and totally kills it, then does such a good job in his match that the architect of the modern-day pro wrestling business gives him the thumbs-up. Not a bad twenty-four hours for a journeyman performer, I'd say!

When the bout ended, I did a little research and found out that James wasn't a clued-out rookie like I'd first thought. He'd actually been working in the business for years as Jimmy Dream, and even owned his own promotion in Maryland. But after years of probably being laughed out of the building when he told people he was a wrestler, he finally got some WWE vindication and a new cult following along with it. I was definitely on Team Ellsworth, as I pitched to Vince to bring him back (he brought him back a half dozen times and eventually signed him to a multi-year contract!) and invited him to guest on *Talk Is Jericho*.

After the show, I asked one of the referees to find James's number and gave him a call. When he answered, I complimented him on his work and congratulated him on his success that night.

I could tell he was a little awestruck to hear from me, but I was happy for him and wanted to give him one last moment to add to his already amazing day.

I wanted to give him The Gift of Jericho. Drink it in, Jaaaaaames!

CHAPTER 18

THE
GENE
SIMMONS
PRINCIPLE

ALWAYS LOOK LIKE A STAR
(OR SPEND MONEY
TO MAKE MONEY)

They come runnin' just as fast as they can,
cause every girl crazy 'bout a sharp dressed man . . .
—ZZ TOP, "SHARP DRESSED MAN"

There's a scene in the riveting Quiet Riot documentary *Now You're Here, There's No Way Back,* where bass player Chuck Wright, wearing a studded-leather jacket, multiple chain bracelets, and a fashionable fedora, is browsing through a rack of shirts in a rock 'n' roll clothing store and proclaims, "Gene Simmons once told me that you should look like a star whenever you leave the house." Makes sense, as I can't envision seeing the Demon walking down the street in gym shorts and flip-flops, can you?

I remembered reading that same Gene quote in *Circus* magazine when I was a teenager (I had a subscription and never missed an issue), and his words made intuitive sense to me. No matter where you are, there's a certain allure to seeing someone walk by who is dressed to kill (and I ain't talkin' about Gene Simmons . . . no wait, yes I am); it gives them a special mystique and makes you think, *Who is that?*

Gene has that mystique in spades and every time I see him in person or on TV, his suits, sunglasses, leather jackets, and spider bracelets (like the one he wore in the Shandi video) make him look like a rock god of thunder.

I agreed with Gene's point and bought into his mindset right from the start of my wrestling career. While most of the other guys wrestling around Calgary in the early '90s were wearing biker shorts and cheap volleyball pads, I scoured the city looking for the best seamstresses to custom make flashy, tassel-festooned (great word) tights, and ordered Trace knee pads (that I still wear) direct from the factory. It took a lot of effort and money that I didn't have, but I always had Gene's attitude that if you wanna be treated like a star, you have to look like one.

I was spending far more money than I was making on that gear, but I always had the best ring costumes on the Alberta independent scene and almost became known for that. I had the same attitude outside the ring, as even though I was twenty years old and mostly broke, I still made it a point to wear cowboy boots with spurs, black bolero hats, dark purple dress shirts with the sleeves rolled up, and a dozen multicolored friendship bracelets every time I went out. The fact that I looked like a total dork to some was completely beside the point: the goal was to stand out from the crowd, and my early '90s rocker look achieved that.

As my career continued, I abided by the "look like a star" rule even more. The most famous example of me going the extra mile to stand out was the debut of my lighted jacket back in 2012, and suffice it to say, the ten thousand dollars (the fifteen thousand dollars I claimed it cost on *Raw* was a slight exaggeration) I spent to have it made has been earned back (avenged) sevenfold over the past five years. It helped me reinvent my character and propel my legacy in the WWE to new heights.

But that's not the only example. When I was "hypocrite" Jericho in 2008, I spent thousands of dollars on Hugo Boss suits, and even though it was a pain in the assski carting them around the world, those suits were a major part of the gimmick's makeup and helped differentiate me from the rest of the pack. I've reinvented my character many times since then, and now I spend good chunks of change on John Varvatos vests and scarves. Those bad boys ain't exactly cheap, but those damn scarves have now become my trademark, so I don't mind spending the cash on them.

The mandate to look like a star at all times is the reason I instituted a "no shorts, baseball caps, or watches onstage" policy for Fozzy, as there's only one band in the world that can get away with wearing street clothes in concert and they're called AC/DC. Even Angus Young runs around in a full velvet schoolboy uniform, complete with a cap embroidered with an "A," an iconic look that everybody knows.

Now, it might take a lot of money and effort to look your best, but it's part of your job if you want to make an impression on people. In this modern era, age is just a number and as long as you try to keep up your appearance, you can stay relevant pretty much until the day you die. I'm not saying you should go for the full-blown Cher and make your face look like an alien cat, but you should do what you can to be in shape and look as hip as possible.

The epitome of this is the Rolling Stones, who still rock and look twenty years younger onstage, even though they are well into their seventies. Mick's flashy jackets and Keith's scarves and headbands automatically make them look larger than life. It's just like putting on a pair of sunglasses: they can instantly transform you into looking like a star. I'm sure that's the reason why Bono, Slash, and Ozzy wear them constantly. Seeing them without their omnipresent shades would be like seeing Hillary Clinton without a pantsuit. It just wouldn't seem right.

Gene is another cat who wears his shades just about every time he's in public and that makes sense to me, given that he's spent the better part of forty-five years in makeup. I'm sure he feels almost naked without the classic Demon design on his face, and the sunglasses allow him to still hide behind the mask, so to speak.

Gene was wearing black wraparound shades when I first met him at the Golden Gods Awards in Los Angeles in 2010, and again when I saw him at the grand opening of the Rock & Brews restaurant in Oviedo, Florida, a few years later. The restaurant was the latest addition to the chain of rock 'n' roll–themed eateries that Gene and Paul Stanley owned. They were both at the opening dressed to the nines in standard rock star duds: black-leather pants and jackets, sport coats, shades, earrings, jewelry hanging off every limb, and of course . . . scarves.

I was wearing a snazzy Varvatos scarf-vest combo myself, as I had been invited to the party by Paul and wanted to look sharp for the occasion. The grand opening was a blast, and Paul and Gene were over-the-top friendly, greeting fans, playing songs on old out-of-tune acoustic guitars (Paul chose "Wild Thing" for some odd reason), and suggesting their favorite items on the menu. We had just finished a great lunch and were hanging out with a mob of fans, when a cute girl came over and asked to take a picture of Gene and me. My best friend and critically acclaimed *Talk Is Jericho* guest Speewee was with me, as he had recently suffered an ugly breakup and had come to Tampa to try to get over his heartache. I asked him to snap the shot and right before did, I mentioned to Gene that it just so happened to be Speewee's birthday.

"What, it's his birthday?" Gene said with mock surprise, holding his hands up to his face like a curmudgeonly Macaulay Culkin. "HIS birthday? Well . . . I don't GIVE A SHIT."

The crowd hushed awkwardly as Speewee and I smiled uncomfortably at each other, not knowing what to do. Finally, Gene said, "I'm just kidding! Happy birthday! Now come here . . ."

He put his hands on each side of Speewee's face and approached him for what looked to be a passionate kiss (no pun intended this time). Spee was agog as the Demon pulled him in like a groom about to smooch his bride for the first time. To make things even creepier, just as he was within target range of Speewee's lips, Gene opened his mouth and released his Kraken-like tongue.

It was an intimidating sight and reminded me of the scene in *Alien 3* when the huge creature gets in Ripley's grill, and the smaller slimy head slides out of its jaws to lick her face. Speewee tried to recoil in shock, but Gene had him in a vice grip and he had no choice but to play along, so he opened his pie-hole to receive The Tongue.

To this day, Speewee claims that Gene's protuberance entered his gob (it didn't), but whether it did or didn't is irrelevant. That's because a few days later Speewee went back to Calgary and went on a major hot streak with the ladies, which he claims was a direct result of his close encounter with the Demon. He swears to this day that when Gene Simmons's tongue went in his mouth, it gave him his mojo back. Well, if that's the case, it's worth a deuce!

Thankfully, I didn't have to kiss the guy from KISS to get him to do my podcast, because after Paul's appearance on *Talk Is Jericho,* the whole KISS camp became enamored with my interview skills and encouraged Gene to do the show next.

After a few back and forth emails, we set a date and agreed to meet at 10 a.m. a few days later at a location of his choice. He sent me an address and told me to meet him at "Bob Goodman's," which seemed a little strange to me. Who exactly was this Bob Goodman? A manager? A friend? Or was it the name of a restaurant or a country club? I wasn't sure, but it didn't matter; I was going to show up promptly at 10 a.m. to interview him, even if we were in the middle of a damn cornfield.

On the morning of the big event, I was up at eight so I could take a shower and fix my hair. After all, I was going into the Demon's den and wanted to make sure I showed up looking like a star. I selected a tight black T-shirt, black vest, swank black-leather boots, and a silver scarf to complete the ensemble . . . on that morning, *Dressed to Kill* wasn't just the name of a KISS album, my friends.

As I drove down a tree-lined street in Hollywood towards Bob Goodman's place, I was as nervous as hell or hallelujah. After all, this wasn't just another interview for my show . . . I was going to be talking to one of the most iconic musicians and pop culture icons of the twenty-first century, who could eat up a journalist and spit him out like fake blood. But I was prepared because after thirty years of being a KISS fan, my goal was to ask him about things he didn't usually get to talk about, and make sure he had a good time chatting with me.

As I drove down the crowded Hollywood streets, the GPS on my phone showed that I was near my destination, and I slowed down as the numbers on the sides of the street moved closer to my target. I pulled up to a short driveway that led up to a big fortress wall, like something you would see in *The Walking Dead,* and assumed that Bob Goodman's compound/restaurant/teenage dance club resided behind it.

I pressed the silver button on the entry box that was window level with my rental car. A female voice answered and I explained that I was there to see Mr. Simmons. After a few seconds, the gate rumbled open to reveal a majestic palace on top of a hill in front of me. You never would've known that the mansion was there from the unassuming gate on the road, but Bob Goodman's place was a real beaut. I figured this Goodman cat was an associate of Gene's who out of the goodness of his heart was allowing us to track the show inside his not so humble abode, and that was okay by me.

I pulled my rental car up a windy driveway, parked at the top, and grabbed my pillowcase full of recording gear. Why do I cart around my expensive and sensitive portable recording studio in a nondescript white pillowcase, you ask? I don't really know, but let's just say that's it's convenient and travels well, okay, junior?

I crossed the driveway until I reached a flight of stairs, and standing at the top like the phantom of the park was Gene Simmons. He of course was fully suited and booted even at such an early hour, wearing a dashing red sports coat with a matching pocket kerchief, snakeskin boots, the obligatory black shades and his helmet of hair perfectly coiffed. He must've gotten up as early as I did to get ready, but I'm sure that was par for the course. He had an interview to do and part of being interviewed was looking your best, no matter what time it was. I was silently inspired as I reached out to shake Gene's hand.

"You have something on your arm," he said slowly in a calm deep voice, as he pumped my hand a few times.

"Huh?" I said confused.

"Your arm. There's a bunch of stuff on it," he said looking at my sleeve of tattoos. "You should wash it off."

I smiled as if my dad had just told a joke, as Gene walked me in to the mansion. The place was even more beautiful on the inside than the outside, with large vaulted ceilings and expensive art on every wall. The foyer was completely spotless and barren, with the only decoration being a life-size statue of a butler. Noticing that I was staring at the sculpture, Gene gave me a helpful tip.

"That's Jeeves. If you go touch his face, he will perform a magic trick for you."

Expecting Jeeves to fart on me or tell me to fuck off, I grabbed the sides of his mug the same way Gene had grabbed Speewee's kisser a few months earlier.

As soon as my hands touched the butler's plastic face, Gene poked my ribs hard and let out a "hee-hee" like the Pillsbury Doughboy.

I jumped around and saw him smiling a Cheshire grin, pleased with himself for tricking me with his literal rib. It seemed odd that he had opened our meeting with a few gags straight from a Henny Youngman Borscht Belt comedy show, but it all made sense later on when he told me he was a huge fan of the old-school comedian.

I was still wondering where Bob Goodman was, but the more I explored the house and the KISS memorabilia covering the walls, I realized this wasn't Bob Goodman's house . . . it was Gene's.

I asked him why he had been so secretive about the whole thing.

"This is your house, Gene. Why did you tell me it was Bob Goodman's?"

Gene gazed at me with a deadpan look and replied, "Well, I couldn't give you my actual address and tell you to meet me at my own house, could I?"

I was pretty sure he could've, plus he had given me his home address regardless, but I went with it anyway.

"But why Bob Goodman? It's such a random name."

"Exactly. It's so average that you would never question it. I was hiding in plain sight."

Umm, okay, Gene.

I laughed to myself how this was going to make a great story in my next book (was I right?) as Gene led us into the living room. He then showed me a wooden box filled to the brim with Purple Heart medals he'd received as gifts from soldiers, thanking KISS for helping to keep them alive during war conditions. I was quite impressed with the significant treasures, but that was just the beginning.

We walked to the other side of the house and up a small flight of stairs into a giant room that could only be described as the greatest KISS museum ever. Every inch was occupied with every item of KISS merch you could possibly imagine, from the '70s to the present. Large glass cabinets lined the walls, stocked with dolls, stuffed animals, lighters, Frisbees, puzzles, eight-track tapes, Colorforms (I loved those when I was a kid), condoms AND coffins ("We get you coming and going," Gene quipped), comics, toys, and masks—all of them emblazoned with the KISS logo or the iconic characters of the Catman, Starchild, Spaceman, and of course the Demon, who was currently standing in front of me explaining the details of the KISS credit card that boasted the latest chip technology.

I took another look around, then pulled my head out of my thirty years of being a KISS fan ass and got down to business. I set up my portable rig and we sat in that marvelous museum for the next ninety minutes talking about KISS, horror movies, the Beatles, Henny Youngman, Japanese meat pies, and setting fans aflame, until I had to regretfully wrap things up to go to my next interview.

Before I left, Gene asked how old my kids were and put together a fine selection of KISS swag for them that included a pillow from a recent KISS Kruise, official New York Yankees–themed shirts featuring all four members dressed in Bronx Bomber regalia, a stuffed animal Demon doll, and a KISS tour program from 2005 (not sure why my kids would want that, but I sure as hell did). He put the souvenirs into a plastic bag with the KISS logo emblazoned on it (of course), and walked me to the foyer.

I shook his hand and thanked him but before I could leave, Gene had a parting comment for me.

"You look really sharp this morning, like a star. I appreciate that."

I hope so, Gene . . . after all, you were the one who taught me about that in the first place.

CHAPTER 19

THE STEVE AUSTIN PRINCIPLE

SOMETIMES YOU HAVE TO BE AN ASSHOLE

I ain't no nice guy after all . . .
—MOTÖRHEAD, "I AIN'T NO NICE GUY"

I was watching a random WWE DVD a few years ago and in the midst of all the talking heads waxing poetic, Stone Cold Steve Austin, possibly the most popular performer in WWE history, said something I'll never forget: "If you want to get ahead in the wrestling business, you have to be a little bit of an asshole."

I picked up what Steve was laying down, but I understand his words even more today, and they don't just apply to the WWE. He wasn't suggesting that you should be a bully tripping nerds while they're carrying trays of food through the cafeteria or kicking a small puppy when you're angry. His message was that you can't be afraid to stand up for yourself when it's necessary, even if you have to show some attitude. Especially within the confines of the WWE, where you need to be willing to ruffle a few feathers to get what you want at times.

For example, I've never had a problem telling the various WWE writers I've worked with that their suggested verbiage simply didn't work for me. I still get a kick out of crumpling up the sheet of paper given to me and tossing it in a junior writer's face (tongue in cheek of course). I'll admit, it's arrogant in theory, but it's become a tradition and always draws a laugh. In reality, the act forces both the writer and myself to get more creative and write something better.

I refuse to accept mediocrity when it comes to my performances within the WWE (or anywhere else), and I don't like being told what to say with a regimented script. But it's my blunt honesty that's helped take me to the top, and I've formed some great partnerships with the writers and producers along the way. I love working behind the scenes with Pat Patterson or Jamie Noble when I'm putting together my matches, because I don't have to worry about hurting their feelings or making them mad if I don't agree with their ideas. I can be straight-up honest about not liking something they suggest and vice versa, which creates a better working environment all around.

During my 2016 WWE run, I started working with a new writer named Chris Scoville, who had wrestled for years on the indie circuit as Jimmy Jacobs. I'd never met him before and even though I'm usually reticent to work with new people, I liked his attitude and after a few successful promo segments, I requested to work with him exclusively. But in order to get truly comfortable working together, I had to be a little abrasive at first. Nothing major, but just enough to let him know that certain ideas presented to me weren't up to snuff. We hammered away on the various scripts, and after a month or so, got on the same page (pun intended again) and became a great writing team. Had

I been worried about hurting his feelings or rubbing him the wrong way, we wouldn't have achieved the same success.

I put together my matches in the same way, and I'm reminded of this every time I reminisce with The Big Show about our time as WWE tag team champions. We were a great combination, as his size and power were the perfect match for my speed and wily heel cowardice. We had a great time in and out of the ring, but as you learned in chapter 15, I was very shall we say . . . persuasive . . . when we were discussing ideas for our matches.

It was frustrating for him for sure, but I still felt there was no reason to use a lesser idea just to appease someone's ego. Show says I'm not difficult to put together a match with, as long as you realize that I'm always right. In my defense, I'd like to retort that he's one hundred percent correct. ;)

I'd also like to point out that I don't care who thinks of the ideas; all that matters is the quality of the match. I feel the same way when it comes to writing a song. While I write the lion's share of Fozzy's lyrics, I hadn't written a single word on two of our biggest hits, "Enemy" and "Lights Go Out." "Lights" is by far our most popular song, a top-20 rock radio hit (and top 10 on the strip club DJ charts . . . which I had no idea even existed), and I didn't contribute a thing to its creation besides the vocals. But as long as the song is good and it rocks, who cares who wrote it? Can you tell me who penned "Back in Black"? No? Well there you go! (It was Angus Young, Malcolm Young, and Brian Johnson, by the way.)

Fozzy works incredibly well as a team, but like most bands with a sizeable fan base, we're not for everybody. To this day, we still get the occasional poor review and I've learned to take the criticism in stride, but sometimes I'll see a review so ricockulous that my Inner Asshole is forced to appear. Especially when the review in question compares us to a leafy vegetable.

Allow me to explain, Constant Reader. Bloodstock is an up-and-coming festival in England that's famous for having a much heavier lineup than the much bigger Download or Sonispshere. In 2013, the promoters were excited to book us for the first time, and it was a great opportunity for us to play a new summer festival in one of our biggest markets.

It was a thrashy lineup that day, as we were slotted in between Exodus and Anthrax, with Slayer headlining the bill. But one of our strengths as a band is that we can gig with anybody due to the diversity of our material, so we knew we'd have to heavy up our set. However, it's no secret that our vibe is more 1979 Van Halen than 1989 Megadeth, and I can honestly say we were the only band who led a "Hey Hey Hey, 1-2-3" chant during the festival. So even though the Bloodstock crowd was more inclined to do a wall of death than a flashing of tits, we had a good show and got a good reaction.

That's why I was so surprised when I read the review of our show in the following month's *Metal Hammer* magazine. It was a typical paint by the numbers burial filled with incorrect details, which made me wonder if the writer had even watched our show. But the coup de grâce was the final line of the report that read: "Fozzy are heavy as lettuce."

Heavy as lettuce? Ouch.

It was a laughable quote that reminded me of the "Shit Sandwich" two-word review of Spinal Tap's *Shark Sandwich* album, but it pissed me off all the same. In the UK, music magazines still have a large influence on what the fans think, and considering I had a good relationship with *Metal Hammer* (I'd hosted their awards show multiple times and written articles for them), I thought it was a low blow. There was no way I was going to let that one slide by, so I dialed up my Inner Asshole.

I wasn't sure what kind of revenge I wanted to plot on *Metal Hammer,* until I told my bro M. Shadows from Avenged Sevenfold (a participant in many a great story in my literary classic, *The Best in the World: At What I Have No Idea*) about the snub.

"Dude, you HAVE to mail them a head of lettuce," he said with a laugh. "That'll send them a message."

Shads was right, I had to do something overtly cheeky in response. If it pissed off *Metal Hammer* and they stopped covering

Fozzy, well, if they were gonna compare us to an edible leaf, what did it matter anyway? What else could they say? We were more purple than an eggplant? More sour than a lemon? The salad was in our court and I was going to toss it back with a Serena Williams–level serve.

The first step was to contact my good bud Jack Slade, part of our fantastic UK Fozzy crew, and ask him to buy a head of lettuce and put in a box. Then I typed up a letter to send with it, and after Jack added a bottle of Newman's Own ranch dressing, our care package was ready for delivery.

A few days later, the fine people at one of England's biggest rock magazines received a package containing a browning head of lettuce, a bottle of ranch dressing, and the following message:

Thank you so much, *Metal Hammer* writers, for the review of our performance at Bloodstock! While we've been called the clichéd "woeful" and "dreadful" many times before, we applaud your originality and creativity in referring to us as "Heavy as Lettuce"! So please enjoy this token of our esteem as we look forward to your future reviews and comparisons of our songs to various items of produce. Love, Fozzy

The joke was received well by the *Hammer* guys and on their website they even posted a picture of the box's contents, along with a description of what had prompted the delivery and a brief "Cheers, Lads!" at the bottom.

I appreciated the good-natured reply to the rib and while I respected *Metal Hammer*'s right to say what they wanted about our performance, it sure felt good to fire back with a shot of our own. That's the therapeutic side of being a little bit of a dick: it can clear your mind and make you feel good that you didn't let somebody walk all over you (and I ain't talkin' about Bon Scott).

ONE OF THE best things about the success of *Talk Is Jericho* is that I've been flown out to see bands play and then interview them for my show. While I've had great experiences with Asking Alexandria, Queensryche, Living Color, and my bro Devin Townsend (with whom I won a Juno Award), the worst was with one of my favorite bands, the Scorpions. Now, before I tell this tale I have to stress that the Scorpions themselves couldn't have been nicer; it was their management that screwed the pooch. But as the wise men from Loverboy once said, we "better start from the start."

I'd been trying to get the Scorpions on *TIJ* since I started doing the show, and while I'd been able to land guitarist Matthias Jabs (who was an excellent guest), I'd never been able to land founder Rudolf Schenker or singer Klaus Meine. I'd come close, as I'd booked them twice, but got blown off both times.

After being a two-time Scorpions loser, I decided I'd had my fill of the Teutonic Terrors and stopped pursuing them. Then my magnificent producer, Stacie Parra, called to say that the Scorps wanted to fly me to Vegas AND pay my hotel in order to appear on my show. What? A free trip to Vegas to hang out and see one of my favorite bands play live? It's a dirty horse, but somebody's gotta ride it . . .

The deal was I'd get Klaus and Rudolf for an hour the day of the show and then stick around to watch the gig afterwards. Everything was set up for us to have our chat at around 7 p.m. (which I thought was a little late considering that the gig started at 9 p.m.), so Stacie gave me their management's number to contact for details when I got into town.

I arrived in Vegas and called at about three to find out where we were supposed to meet, but the guy who answered seemed to have no idea who I was. I reminded him about our interview, and with some prodding he finally replied in an annoyed tone, "Okay, well, you can have fifteen minutes with Rudolf at 7 p.m."

Fifteen minutes? Was this a rib? My shortest ever *TIJ* interview was forty minutes with Rob Zombie and without at least that amount of time, I wouldn't have enough material for a show. It didn't make any sense, especially when the band had spent money to bring me in, and I told the guy so.

When I mentioned it had been agreed that I'd have an hour with Rudolf AND Klaus, the dipshit laughed into the earpiece and told me fifteen minutes was the best he could do. What pissed me off even more was that he was acting like he was doing me a favor in allowing me to talk to Rudolf at all. I reiterated that I needed forty minutes minimum and that the Scorps organization had paid for me to be there in the first place.

Dipshit called back a few minutes later and told me to meet the band's rep at the venue at 5:30 p.m. so that when Rudolf got there at 7 p.m., I could get started. Oh, and he was now offering me the princely sum of twenty minutes (I wasn't even gonna hassle the fact that Klaus was apparently no longer involved), because they had a VIP meet and greet at 7:30 p.m. sharp. So in reality I was going to have less than half an hour, which was far too short for a full episode. That meant I was going to have to make the best of it and try to squeeze out more time somehow.

I had taken thirty-minute interview slots and expanded them to forty-five minutes before, by using the subtle asshole technique of ignoring the clock. I got an extra ten minutes with Zombie that way, when I basically tuned out his handler when he came in the room to wrap up the chat. I figured I could do the same thing with Rudolf, or just play it by ear and see what type of mood he was in. Maybe he'd want to talk longer if he was enjoying himself.

When I got to the foyer of the Joint at 5:30 p.m., I was met by a man that I can only describe as the epitome of a dweeb. He was nerdy, socially awkward, and timid: the exact opposite of what you would expect the representative of a massive band like the Scorpions to be.

Let me also say that after being in show business for over twenty-six years, I have a good feel for figuring out a person's true character within minutes of meeting them. And Dweeb Mc-Queen was giving me a bad vibe right from jump street.

"Hi," he mumbled nervously, his eyes darting back and forth around the room. "I guess we should go inside."

Yeah, no shit, Dweeback, unless you just want to hang here in the deserted lobby, looking for change on the carpet?

He led me inside the venue and even though I knew where the dressing room was (I had interviewed Paul Stanley in this exact arena a year prior), this goober didn't seem to know where he was. After walking aimlessly around for ten minutes, I realized that he really had no idea where we were supposed to go. I felt like David St. Hubbins and was about to start shouting, "Hello, Cleveland," when Dweeb Aoki stopped at the top of a flight of stairs and admitted he was lost. I told him that the backstage lounge area was actually at the bottom of the steps and that was probably the best place for me to set my stuff up.

"No!" he snapped. "You'll be setting up in Rudolf's dressing room . . . if I could only remember where it is."

We stood there for a few more seconds until he finally took my advice and walked down the stairs. When he got to the bottom and swung open the door to the lounge, Dweebil Zappa announced, "This . . . is the LOUNGE!"

Then he told me he would come get me when Rudolf arrived and disappeared behind the door, leaving me with no pass, no ticket, and no credentials.

So instead of setting up my rig in Rudolf's dressing room and being ready to start the second he arrived, I stood there and twiddled my thumbskis for the next thirty minutes. I hung around like a fanboy until a security guard came by and asked for my credentials, which of course I didn't have. Thankfully, he knew who I was and what I was there for ("Recording a podcast today, Chris?"), which put him two steps above Dweeb Harris, who still hadn't returned.

When the clock hit 7 p.m. I was about to abort the mission, until the door opened and Dweebee Cates summoned me inside with no words of explanation or apologies as to why I'd been left out there for so long. We walked through the catacombs of the backstage area and down a hallway to a door with a RUDOLF sign plastered on it.

I walked inside and there was Rudolf Schenker, the legendary founder of the Scorpions sitting on a couch. He looked trim and considerably younger than his sixty-seven years, and couldn't have been more friendly as I set up my Zoom recorder and microphones. Just before I pressed record, Justin Dweeber said in a fake friendly voice, "So about twenty minutes then?"

Yeah, fat chance of that, I thought to myself as I smiled and started the interview.

For the next twenty minutes Rudolf was a tremendous guest. I could tell he was genuinely engaged in our conversation about rock 'n' roll fashion, the 1983 US Festival, why he shaved his trademark moustache, and the 1989 Moscow Music Peace Festival. After twenty minutes, like clockwork, the Dweebler Elf came in about as silent as an asthmatic rhino, but since Rudolf didn't acknowledge his shitty handler's existence, I didn't either. Finally, Stacy Dweebler waved his hands over his head in a panic, mouthing, "Five more minutes!" He wasn't happy but I didn't give a shit, because Rudolf was on a roll and I now had twenty-seven minutes in the can.

I was almost home free.

But a few minutes later, Dipshit made his big return by barging into the dressing room, and both he and Dweeb Schreiber pointed at their nonexistent watches and shook their fingers angrily until finally Dweeba McIntyre stood up and yelled, "That's it, Rudolf has to go! You're finished here!"

I was really getting sick of these guys treating me like I was a high school journalist who'd won an "Interview the Scorpions" contest in the local newspaper. But out of respect to Rudolf, who had treated me so well, I decided to back off and let it go with just over thirty minutes in the can. It was a short interview, but it was really good and I would make it work somehow. I thanked him, but just as I was getting ready to leave, Rudolf said in his charming German accent, "Why don't you sink of sree or fouh more questionz and we can continue when I'm done with ze meet and greet?"

I was ecstatic and told him I'd be waiting for him the moment he got back. Rudolf shook my hand and told me to make myself at home as he and Dipshit walked out of the room. I was left alone with Steve Dweebee, who was staring a hole through me like he had caught me taking a dump in his mom's kitchen sink.

"You want me to wait outside?" I said cheerfully, knowing damn well he'd heard Rudolf tell me to make myself at home.

"That would be best," Robert Louis Dweebenson replied acerbically.

What was he expecting me to do, walk out with one of Schenker's famous flying Vs stuffed down my pants? But okay, whatever, never mind, I walked the five steps across the hall to the Scorpions' drummer (and my bro) Mikkey Dee's room and killed some time watching *Judge Judy*. A few minutes later I saw Rudy walking back into his room, and even though I was on the edge of my seat waiting to see if Judge Judy was going to allow some poor guy to break his lease because the house he was renting had no working stove and an ant infestation (hope things worked out for him), I went and knocked on Rudy's door. He was all smiles and we immediately picked up the conversation right where we left off.

"Okay, Rudolf, we were in the middle of a fantastic chat when your handlers cut us off . . ."

". . . Yes, along with ze police and ze Gestapo," he added comically.

He totally got the ridiculousness of the situation and with good vibes in the air we continued our conversation. I can say that the second part was just as good as the first . . . until Stone Cold Dweeb Austin cut us off again after a mere seven minutes.

He was pissed that I had come back into Rudy's dressing room without his "permission," even although he was sitting right there when Rudy made the offer to continue with me in the first place.

"I told you this interview is over! You're done!" he bellowed belligerently.

That was it. I was sick of this little jackoff talking to me like a mark and was going to tell him so, but first I thanked Rudolf for a great interview. He reciprocated and asked me to contact him the next time I was in Hanover, so he could come see me perform in return. We shook hands and when he left to get ready for the show, I set my sights back on Dweebo Bryson and glared into his beady eyes.

"I know you heard Rudolf tell me to come back and continue my interview after his meet and greet. So I'd say you were pretty fuckin' rude right there, don't you think?"

"Well, Rudolf shouldn't have said that and besides, you gotta get out of here. I have a show to run."

He began rushing me out of the room, even though I still had to pack up my recording gear. The breaking point had been reached and out came The Inner Asshole.

"HEY!" I said gruffly. "You need to back off, dude. The Scorpions spent some good money to bring me out here, so quit acting like you're doing me a fucking favor and get out of my face. Do you understand?"

Dweeby Harry's eyes got as big as saucers and he appeared to be on the verge of crying.

"Do. You. Understand. Me?" I said, enunciating each word, so even his stupid ass would understand.

He nodded and walked out of the room quickly. Feeling satisfied with myself, I packed up my stuff and went down to the box office to pick up my passes for the show, but to the surprise of exactly no one, Dweebus Christ hadn't left me a damn thing. The dude working the box office was totally cookie and said even though the show was sold out, he'd figure something out. At that moment, as if on cue, Brutus "The Barber" Dweebcake walked in the box office and practically bumped right into me.

"Hey, man . . ." he mumbled, looking like he was going to poop his pantskis, ". . . everything all right?"

"Actually, there's no ticket or pass for me here. This dude offered to help me out, but since you asked, maybe you can take care of it."

"Aww, man, the pass was supposed to be there, but it's a sold-out show. Guess there's nothing I can do."

Why would he be able to do anything, he was only the handler of the fucking headlining band! But then I had an idea.

"Why don't you give me your pass?"

"My pass? But this is all access."

"Yeah, I see that, it's perfect. So why don't you give it to me and then go upstairs and get another one?"

I stared him down as he considered his options, his wheels spinning. I think he was genuinely intimidated by The Inner Asshole and in the end smartly decided to cut his losses with me. He defeatedly slid the lanyard over his head and slowly handed over his pass.

"This should take care of it," he muttered. Then he dodged inside the door of the venue and stammered, "I'll be right back."

Of course you will, Junior, I thought to myself, but of course he didn't come back and I never saw him again. And apparently the Scorpions never saw him again after the tour either, because I heard they fired his ass after the last show.

The moral of the story is that by unleashing The Inner Asshole and standing my ground with Cheryl Dweebs, I ended up with a wicked thirty-seven-minute interview with Rudolf Schenker (just long enough for a full show), and with my all-access pass I got to see the Scorpions tear Las Vegas apart from the front row. All in all, it was a pretty rad day at the office.

The moral of the story is if some stupid idiot is trying to push you around, don't be afraid to show some attitude, stand your ground, and rock them like a hurricane.

Or at least take their all-access pass.

CHAPTER 20

THE BOWIE PRINCIPLE

REINVENT YOURSELF

Ch-ch-changes, turn and face the strange,
Oh look out you rock 'n' rollers . . .
—DAVID BOWIE, "CHANGES"

A few years ago, the WWE asked me to talk about The Under-taker and his longevity within the company for a special they were producing. After waxing poetic on his legendary gimmick and ring prowess, I commented that he was "the David Bowie of the wrestling business." At first that might seem like a strange way to describe The Deadman, Constant Reader, but once you hear my whole theory I'm sure you'll agree it makes sense.

Ever since Bowie released his first album and became a star (man) in 1969, he changed his look and sound on every record he released until his death in 2016. From *Ziggy Stardust*'s androg-ynous alien rock star, to the drug-addled Thin White Duke of the mid-'70s , to the well-dressed lothario of the *Let's Dance* era, he constantly altered his style and musical vision. Every album still sounded like Bowie at the root, but contained an updated, rebooted version of himself with each new release. Now if you really think about it, throughout the years The Undertaker has shared the same metamorphosis.

From his debut in 1990 as the white-faced, red-haired walking corpse, to the goateed Satanic priest of the Attitude Era, to the American Bad Ass motorcycle man of the early 2000s, to the MMA-influenced streetfighter gimmick he ended his career with (or did he?), Mark Calaway constantly evolved his character and stayed meaningful. There might be certain eras of The Undertaker that we like better, but much like KISS, Aerosmith, or the Stones, Taker did what he had to do to keep his character fresh, interesting, and most importantly, RELEVANT.

How many times have you watched a wrestling show, music video, or HBO comedy special and queried, "This guy is still around . . . and doing the same old shtick?" Well, in the spirit of Lazarus and The Phenom, I vowed I would never be that same old guy, doing the same old shit.

I strived to change my look, my catchphrases, my moves, and my character as much as I could, which was important considering I was on television twice a week, every week. Pat Patterson used to marvel at my weekly facial hair changes in the early 2000s, a tactic I used to keep my image fresh. Changing even such a small detail helped me to stay creatively stimulated and gave me a different look from show to show.

If I didn't change things up, people would see the same Chris Jericho 104 times a year, and that would get boring fast. Soon, that changing of my facial hair expanded to my hair style, my wrestling gear, my raps on the way to the ring, everything. It was a smart move both from a "keeping it fresh" standpoint and from a business one as well, because the more pairs of tights I wore, the more action figures they made of me. There are over two hundred different tiny versions of me now; how many of them do you have? Go ahead and check, I'll wait.

Wow, that many, huh? You are a true Friend of Jericho!

Anyway, making constant ch-ch-ch-changes is the only way I can operate, even though it makes some people mad. I constantly hear complaints from fans telling me to grow my hair out and go back to wearing suits and long tights or calling people hypocrites, but my answer is always the same: "Been there, done that."

Why would I want to go back to the past to try to re-create something that's outlived its shelf life? Once I've created a new character, to go back to the old one would be like putting on a used condom. It might still fit, but it would feel warped, uncomfortable . . . and, well, disgusting.

This is not just a principle for show business; it's a rule that can be applied to any business or aspect of your life. If something isn't working or is getting stale, then it's time to reinvent and modify, no matter if it's your relationship, job, living arrangements, car, favorite pair of jorts, you name it. Whatever it is, you have to keep things fresh, (and I ain't talkin' about Kool & the Gang) if you want to stay relevant.

That's been the method to my madness ever since I debuted in the WWE in 1999. There have been so many different looks, costumes, catchphrases, gimmicks, and coifs, but which one was your favorite? Here's a quick rundown to help refresh your memory . . .

Y2J Jericho—(1999): This was the original incarnation of the character that made me famous. Brash, obnoxious, full of ego—and that was just behind the scenes. The trademark of this guy was long blond hair with a carefully constructed topknot (which I stole from *Hotter Than Hell*–era Gene Simmons), a look that's still popular now. I get at least one tweet a day from somebody posting a picture of themselves or their kid sporting the "Y2J topknot." It makes me laugh, because I only wore the damn thing for about six months before I switched it to a back-of-the-head ponytail (which I stole from *Revenge*-era Gene Simmons). I guess you just never know what's going to stick in a Jerichoholic's mind!

The look was completed with a scraggly goatee, a silver rave shirt, a pair of tight leather pants, and a jangly chain belt. The chin pubes were quickly shaved off, but the rave shirts lasted for a few years before being replaced by sparkly pajama tops with matching bottoms (the most famous maroon-pink version of which still reeks of stale beer due to taking a summer's worth of stunners from Stone Cold Steve Austin).

The catchphrases of the time were mostly retreads from WCW, including "Jerichoholics," "Welcome to Raw Is Jericho," "Never EEEVVVEEERRR Be the Same Agayn," and "I Am the Ayatollah of Rock 'n' Rollah," with "Would You Please Shut the Hell Up?" and "King of the World" added in over the next few years.

Bearded Jericho—(2003): At this point, I had grown back the long King Tut goatee, the result of a beard-growing contest with Zakk Wylde (I obviously lost), and I wore my long blond hair in a variety of ponytails, braids, and man buns. I had dyed the tips red (I stole that from Ozzy Osbourne), which left a bloody-looking mess in the shower that resembled the opening scene in *Carrie* whenever I had to recolor them. The sparkly beer-soaked ring pajamas were replaced by red velvet pants with a weird Cossack design and a matching short-sleeved dressy shirt with red lips printed all over it. The catchphrases were "Assclown," "Larger Than Life," and the drinking of "Jerichohol."

Bowlcut Jericho—(2005): It had to happen eventually, but it was not a popular decision when I finally cut my hair. I went from having long, majestic, chest-length locks to a shoulder-length bob, which left me looking like I was wearing a bell on my head. I mean, I had friends; why didn't they tell me how bad my Darth Vader hair helmet looked? Eventually, I cut it shorter to where it looked vaguely Beatle-esque, and while that was better than the Hanson lid I'd been sporting, it still wasn't stylish . . . unless you were Ringo Starr in 1965.

The velvet pants were replaced by long wrestling tights made out of a weird velvet material that never quite fit, along with a matching satin pajama-style ring jacket. The new catchphrases included "Sexy Beast," "You Can't Stop Rock 'n' Roll . . . and You Can't Stop Chris Jericho Either" and "Vitamin C."

Save Us Jericho—(2007): After a twenty-seven-month hiatus, I returned to the WWE in November of 2007 with a series of cryptic vignettes that claimed someone or something was coming to "save" the company. These ran for over two months until I finally made my big redebut as the man who was going to "save us" from all the awful things that had happened recently in the WWE, including the coronation of World Champion Randy Orton. This incarnation of Jericho boasted an even shorter spiky haircut, which once again left a lot of fans unhappy. Y2J without long hair was the equivalent of James Hetfield or Jaimie Lannister with a beaner . . . the same guy, just not as dashing, tough, or cool looking. The long hair was so tied in with the Jericho persona that Don Callis even asked me if I was going to come back with extensions.

"How can you be Chris Jericho without long hair?"

I didn't think it would matter, but I still wanted to keep the rest of the Y2J gimmick intact, so I wore a shiny silver vest, a wife beater, and a wallet chain (a look inspired by Sting's stage wear on the Police reunion tour). I also had a new finisher called the "Codebreaker" that I had seen used as a transition maneuver in Japan and stole for myself. I didn't have any new catchphrases besides "Save Us" and maybe "Me Want Title Match" (a minor hit only familiar to the diehards, like the Jericho equivalent of KISS's "Turn On the Night"). A new version of my theme song (recorded by Zakk Wylde) was rejected by Vince, so I went back to the same one I'd been using since my WWE debut eight years earlier. But even with a new finish and a semi-new image, this character wasn't that much different from 2005 Bowlcut Jericho, and my act quickly became stagnant. Thankfully, I knew it and reinvented myself into what was one of the top two most critically acclaimed characters of my career.

Suit & Tie Guy Evil Jericho—(2008): It was well documented in my most excellent codex *Best in the World: At What I Have No Idea* how this manifestation of Jericho was inspired by a combination of Anton Chigurh from the Coen brothers' *No Country for Old Men* and late-'70s AWA Nick Bockwinkel. The character was a career changer for me and led to what was possibly the best run of my career. This guy exclusively wore a suit and tie and spoke in a low, emotionless voice that forced the entire audience to shut up and pay attention to what he was saying, which was no mean feat in the post–Stone Cold Steve Austin "What" world. I also peppered my speech with what my auntie Joan called "five-dollar words," multisyllable idioms that pissed the audience off by going over their heads. The catchphrases at this time were a confluence (five-dollar word) of insults thrown at the audience, such as "Hypocrites," "Troglodytes," "Sycophants," and "Gelatinous Tapeworms" (my personal favorite), along with the debut of the "I'm the best in the world at what I do; do you understand what I'm saying to you right now?" maxim that I still use. I also made another controversial decision and switched from long tights to short trunks, which once again gets me complaints to this day. HEY, YOU NEED TO CHANGE BACK TO TIGHTS, BECAUSE THOSE TRUNKS MAKE YOU LOOK LIKE YOU HAVE A DAD BOD, said @dinkus96. Hmmm, well, since I have three kids AND a bod, I guess that's an apt description.

The traction I got from this character due to my classic feuds with Shawn Michaels, Rey Mysterio, and DX (with Big Show as my partner) cemented my legacy in the WWE and took me to a level I hadn't been before. Had I not taken the chance and reinvented myself, I'd probably be out of wrestling by now, or at the very least having a dog collar match against The Black Mamba in Sweet Lips, Tennessee, next weekend.

I Invented Everything Jericho—(2012): Another hiatus led to another series of cryptic vignettes promoting my return by threatening "The End of the World as We Know It." This all came about when I left the company to do *Dancing with the Stars* and guys like The Miz, CM Punk, and Kofi Kingston started borrowing my look, moves, catchphrases, and promo style. It didn't bother me because I'd stolen most of my stuff from other people in the first place, but I thought it could lead to some good storytelling when I returned. So I accused the entire WWE of copying me, as I had pretty much invented everything the company had ever done that was successful. The new catchphrases were "Copycats" and "Wannabees," which led to the worst Jericho merch shirt in history, featuring a giant Raid can that could be used to kill WannaBEES (sorry if you bought that one). The rest of this guy's wardrobe harkened back to the swank leather pants and studded-leather jackets of earlier years. I also added another integral piece to the character that became as iconic as the Y2J nickname . . . the Lighted Jacket. I was looking for something unique and original to add to my act, but as I mentioned earlier in this folio, they weren't always the easiest props to work with and caused me a ton of hassle. However, they were worth every second of annoyance felt and every dollar spent, because they became my trademark. As a matter of fact, one of the biggest things I miss about being a babyface is the roar of the crowd when that electric bad boy turns on and hundreds of tiny flashing lights pierce the darkness of my entrance. But alas, when I turned heel on AJ Styles in 2016, all the froot babyface tricks had to go, hence the destruction of my poor jacket at the hands of Dean Ambrose.

Return to Y2J Beach—(2013): After four years of heavy heelness, including a two-year stretch where I was the most hated bad guy in the wrestling world, it got quite difficult to elicit boos, so it was time to make the switch back to babyface. This finally took place with no pomp and circumstance whatsoever, when I returned from a thirty-day suspension for kicking a Brazilian flag (read all about this incident in my memoir of international intrigue, *Best in the World*) and morphed into a good guy overnight just by working with the hated Dolph Ziggler and the more despicable Vickie Guerrero. This was the period where I decided it might be a good idea to grow my hair out, but couldn't figure out what to do with it as it got longer, so I just slicked it back with a shield of hairspray. Unfortunately, when that spray loosened up with sweat, the hair fell listlessly to both sides of my head, making me look like a less fashionable William Regal. There were no new catchphrases because I adapted the adage "What's old is new" and just recycled all of my classics. It was fun for the fans to hear them again (once), as I hadn't used them in years, and a blast from the past to bring back my previously retired *Highlight Reel* segment. But like a rock band who tours every summer but never releases a new album, the nostalgia wore off fairly quickly. I did get a new costume design and went with a wicked-looking logo on my tights that said "Y2J 2013," which morphed to "Y2J 2014" the following year and so on. But I kept using the rehashed Y2J for the next two and a half years and everybody, even hardcore Jerichoholics, felt it was getting stale. It was becoming apparent that the goodwill extended to me with each return was getting less every time, as my reactions were lukewarm and online critics were tearing me apart, demanding my retirement. Thankfully, I had been through it all before and knew it was the perfect time to . . . say it with me, kids . . . REINVENT MYSELF!

Stupid Idiot Jericho—(2016): When I came back to the WWE in January of 2016, my idea was to come back as a heel. I wanted to reunite with my old partner Big Show and have him be my heater leading into a feud with Dean Ambrose for WrestleMania 31.

I originally only planned to stay with WWE until the end of April, so turning heel quickly was essential. But then something interesting happened . . . I started to really enjoy myself. Something was different about this run, maybe because since I knew the endgame was for me to turn heel, there was no pressure on me as a babyface. I could say what I wanted and not have to worry if my lines were stale or cheesy (see "Rooty Tooty Booty"), and the plan to slowly piss people off, worked. I instantly got hundreds of tweets saying my work was lame and that my "shirtless with a scarf" outfit looked horrible and douchy:

> Jericho that vest/scarf combo is brutal. Please put a shirt on.
>   —@thegordiecanuck

> Y2J's scarf is the worst thing on Raw. He looks ridiculous and his insults are lame!
>   —TubaBoy257

> Chris Jericho is old and out of place. Take off the scarf, put on a shirt and retire now!
>   —@ClintBobski18

I found it funny that more people were talking about my scarf and lack of shirt than the main event of the next PPV. Once again, I had made the most subtle of changes to my character to get a response, and it had worked like a charm. When I finally turned heel on AJ Styles and called the audience "Stupid Idiots," it drew major heat. When I started using the insult, people hated me for saying it, along with my other new catchphrases, like "The Gift of Jericho," "Quiet," and "It." When I started saying "Drink It In, Maaaan," I would spit out the words, then stand in silence with my arms outstretched and my eyes closed in a euphoric daze, while the fans booed me out of the building. But only a few months later, people were chanting along and wanting "Drink

It In, Maaaan" water bottles and T-shirts at the souvenir stand. There was such a demand that I even broke my "no merch" rule and allowed the WWE to market Jericho swag for the first time in years.

However, it didn't matter that people went from hating the sayings to wanting to wear them on their bodies. The point was I had reinvented myself again and had risen to being one of the top heels and hottest acts in the company as a result. Some would say this was the most popular incarnation of Jericho ever, but that's for you to decide, not me.

I got new tights made with G.O.A.T on the back, which for those of you who aren't hip with the terms of the street like I am, yo, means "Greatest of All Time." Hey, it's hard to be humble when you're perfect in every way, right? I also incorporated a few new moves into my repertoire, including a second-rope enziguri, which I hadn't seen before, and a jumping elbow from the top rope, which I hadn't used in years.

Also due to a good diet, smarter psychology, and DDP Yoga, my body felt great and I had one of my best career runs in the ring as well. I expanded my mindset on how to put together a match after working with guys like Cesaro, Ambrose, Sami Zayn, and Seth Rollins. This newer generation of performers had no problem doing multiple superkicks or dives during a match, which is something I never would've allowed in my matches in the past, because it wasn't the way I usually did things. I always believed that using a move once in a match was enough, but by working with those guys and having an open mind to how the business had evolved, I evolved as well.

Of course the crowning jewel of this era was my storyline with my best friend, Kevin Owens. The chemistry between us was undeniable and lead to an amazing program of over eight months, culminating with my exit from the company in May of 2017. There are many stories from this era involving Kevin, Seth Rollins, Sami Zayn, Roman Reigns, Gallows, Anderson, Braun

Strowman, Brock Lesnar and more, but I'll save those for another time. And don't even get me started on The List of Jericho . . . that deserves an entire book of its own!

Future of Jericho—(2017–???): As I write this primer, I have no idea what the future holds for me as far as my involvement in WWE goes . . . in the words of the great Joe Strummer, "Should I stay or should I go?" Only I can answer that, and as of this writing I'm not sure.

I suspect I'll stay in the business for a while because as long as I can stay healthy, compete at the highest of levels, and have an angle I can sink my teeth into, there's no reason to stop. I don't see why I can't pop in from time to time for many years to come, either as a regular television performer or even just exclusively doing live events like I did in 2015. One thing I know for sure, no matter what my involvement is, if and when I return to the WWE, it will be with a new move, a new look. I'll always continue to reinvent myself, because to paraphrase another entertainment chameleon named Madonna:

"Bitch, I'm Chris Jericho!"

EPILOGUE

GOODBYE...
IF ONLY
FOR NOW

And in the end, the love you take
is equal to the love you make . . .

—THE BEATLES, "THE END"

Well, that's it, Constant Reader. I hope you enjoyed this little treatise and even learned a thing or two. If you walk away from this book with only one lesson learned, let's hope it's this: if you want to make something happen, MAKE IT HAPPEN! From this moment on, let's leave the excuses behind and achieve dem goals, all right?

Remember, when I first moved to Calgary in 1990, away from the comforts of my mom's home, I had no guarantees, no fixed future, and no backup plan. It was all or nothing and nobody was going to tell me any different. I had no money, no job, nowhere to live, a shitty '76 Volare with a full tank of gas, a half a pack of cigarettes, it was dark, and I was wearing sunglasses. But I also had the desire and passion to make things happen and that, along with an impenetrable belief in myself, was all I really needed. I believe that's all YOU really need as well.

So here I am almost twenty-seven years later, and even though I've been blessed by the Lord all across the board, I've also put in the Herculean time and backbreaking effort necessary to accomplish whatever I set my mind to. It hasn't always been easy, but it's been worth it and I wouldn't change a thing, because in the words of Rob Halford, I've got "one life and I'm gonna live it up!"

I did it . . . you can do it.

Love you guys!

Chris Jericho
April 28, 2016–October 2, 2016

ACKNOWLEDGMENTS

Thanks to God for allowing me to write book number four and for always being in my corner. No matter what I do, he's always got my back and I couldn't succeed and survive in this crazy life without him. As always . . . JESUS ROCKS!

Thanks to Jessica, Ash, Cheyenne, and Sierra for loving me and for the sacrifices they face when I'm out making the donuts.

Thanks to Peter Thomas Fornatale, my long time partner in literary crime for helping me edit this book and giving me additional tips, pointers, and valuable advice. Even though I'm all grown up when it comes to writing books, I still need your love, need your love, need your love, need your lovvvvvve . . . (figure that one out!).

Thanks to Ben Schafer and the fine folks at Da Capo Press. Looking forward to a long and FROOTFUL relationship!

Thanks to my awesome agent, Marc Gerald (and his killer assistant Kim Koba), for giving me the great idea for the format of this book. Many more to come, Marc!

Thanks to Christine Marra for helping with the editorial production of this book.

Hope I didn't forget anybody, but if I did...you know what happens? You know what happens when Y2J forgets your name in the acknowledgments of this book? You know what happens if I forgot you? YOU JUST MADE THE LIST!!

Also please remember, anybody spelling the song "Halloween" from the group "Helloween" with an "E" and the group with an "A" will immediately be turned into a big, ugly, half-price–selling pumpkin. That is all.

Up The Irons!